A
VERY BRITISH
REVOLUTION
150 YEARS OF JOHN LEWIS

JONATHAN GLANCEY

LAURENCE KING PUBLISHING

LAURENCE KING

Published in 2014
by Laurence King Publishing Ltd
361–373 City Road
London EC1V 1LR
Tel +44 20 7841 6900
Fax +44 20 7841 6910

enquiries@laurenceking.com
www.laurenceking.com

A catalogue record for this book is
available from the British Library

ISBN: 978-178067-238-0

Design concept: Pentagram

Printed in the UK

A

VERY BRITISH

REVOLUTION

150 YEARS OF JOHN LEWIS

JONATHAN GLANCEY

THE
FIRST
JOHN LEWIS

1864–1914

The fabric departments of John Lewis are, for many customers, the chief glory of these familiar-yet-special shops, which have been run since 1929 as an employee-owned partnership, although founded in rather different circumstances 150 years ago. This is arguably how it should be, for the business was founded by a Victorian draper who specialized in selling fabrics. It is even said that the first John Lewis shop, in London's Oxford Street, stocked 50 shades of black silk to meet the needs of Victorian mourners.

Today's John Lewis shops are very different from their Victorian forebears. Society has moved on in many ways since the 1860s. Values have changed along with dress, manners, accents, social taboos and prohibitions. And so has the nature of shops: today, they are as much about entertainment and enjoyment as they are about measuring exact lengths of fabrics and ensuring that these are the right shade of black. But John Lewis's roots – no matter how the shops have blossomed since – are grounded, quite happily, in drapery and fabrics.

John Lewis was born in the West Country in 1836 – the year before Queen Victoria came to the throne. He was one of several drapers who set up shop in London from the mid-nineteenth century onwards. In doing so, these buyers and sellers of cloth, principally for clothing, created the British department store, a revolution both in retailing and in the social life and order of the Victorian and Edwardian city. Among them were William Whiteley, Arthur Liberty and Peter Jones, all of whom founded shops that were to become famous.

England had always excelled in the wool and fabric trade, whether producing, buying or selling. The fabric of many of its wealthiest towns – their lofty churches, guildhalls, merchants' houses and market crosses – had been founded on *fabric* itself. So, it should be no surprise that the country's drapers were to play such an active and conspicuous role in the Victorian retail revolution. This was itself a product of the Industrial Revolution, which had, at first, threatened and even destroyed the old, 'homespun' ways of making and selling goods and fabrics.

Opposite
Colourfully dressed ladies discuss the latest fabric designs for 1851 from the Yorkshire mills of Titus Salt, at the Great Exhibition.

Above
John Lewis, photographed in 1910, aged 74: every inch the successful Victorian patriarch and entrepreneur.

Drapers played a key role in building London into a fast-growing, rich and immensely powerful global city during Queen Victoria's long reign. Even today, London's fashion business is one of the world's most successful, most innovative and most inspirational.

John Lewis himself, one of six children, was born at home in a handsome three-storey Georgian house in Shepton Mallet, Somerset, in February 1836. His father – also John Lewis, and possibly of Welsh descent – was a baker. His mother, Elizabeth (née Speed), came from a family made comfortably off through a string of local businesses. Although the Lewis family, who had lived in the town since the 1660s, was moderately affluent, Shepton Mallet itself had been through hard times over many years as its traditional wool, cloth and silk industries collapsed under the weight of new forms of manufacturing and international trade.

The looming presence of the town's vast new workhouse, commissioned in 1836 – two years before Charles Dickens published *Oliver Twist* – and the latest additions to the grimly monumental House of Correction, with its hernia-inducing treadmill, were sad reminders of the Industrial Revolution's negative aspects. There were fortunes to be made in new industry and enterprise, but at a high cost to those who, one way or another, were unable to move with the times. This often meant physically relocating to distant cities. As John Lewis grew up, in a family of doting sisters, vast swathes of the rapidly expanding English population moved away from villages and country towns like Shepton Mallet.

The new railways accelerated this unprecedented movement of people. They were also to play a critical, and profitable, role in the rise of new forms of shopping – and the department stores founded by a generation of ambitious Victorian drapers. The first trains arrived in Shepton Mallet in 1858, and for many years the town was served by two stations. These gave direct services to Bath and Bournemouth, Wells and, with a single change

Top
An artist's impression of how the interior of John Lewis may have looked in 1864.

Above
Cover of an 1898 'blotter', for drying the ink on notes and bills, from Bainbridge & Co of Newcastle upon Tyne, depicting leisurely and elegantly spacious shopping. The store was bought by John Lewis in 1953.

Left
Augusta East, Lady Hoare, painted in Paris by Lord Leighton in 1858 when she was 28, in mourning apparently for her husband's late uncle and benefactor.

Below
Even Olivia, Shakespeare's heroine from *Twelfth Night*, painted in 1888 by Edmund Blair Leighton, appears in a take on Victorian mourning dress.

50
SHADES
OF
BLACK

Prince Albert died in 1861, ten years after the hugely successful Great Exhibition. This unprecedented display of goods, and design trends, drawn from around the world had owed much to Prince Albert's initiative and support. Queen Victoria chose to wear black from his death until her own 40 years later, which is why we often associate the colour black, as well as grand funerals and veiled widows mourning, with the Victorian era. This, though, was also a time of widespread infant mortality, of cholera, malnutrition and appalling industrial accidents: funerals were very much a part of everyday life. Of course,

it was also an era of soot, industrial grime and polluted skies. Black, then, was a sensible colour for clothing, and John Lewis, picking up on contemporary fashion and social trends, stocked an extraordinary assortment of black fabrics. It was said that you could buy 50 shades of black at the Oxford Street store. The trade in mourning dress was high, but to dress in black could also be the height of chic. Black fabrics could be lustrous as well as glum, while the sheer variety of materials available in black – from wool and cotton to silk, astrakhan, alpaca and ostrich feathers – was as rich as imperial trade could make it.

of train, to Bristol and London. By then, however, John Lewis had taken his own train to London (from Liverpool, as it happens, where he had been apprenticed) and begun his illustrious career as one of the capital's most successful businessmen.

It had, however, been something of a slog – and a worrying one, too. By 1843, John and his sisters had been orphaned. They were saved from the threat of the workhouse by their Aunt Christian, the eldest of six aunts on the Speed side of the family. Aunt Christian ran a hat shop in Cowl Street, Shepton Mallet. A single and independent woman in her late forties, she took responsibility for the Lewis children, marrying one James Clark (possibly for financial security), who happened to be the Principal Turnkey, or jailer, at the terrifying House of Correction. Widowed by the late 1850s, Aunt Christian set up in the drapery business in Weston-super-Mare, where she continued to look after John's sisters Elizabeth, Mary and Eliza.

Meanwhile, she had enrolled John, at the age of 11, at Shepton Mallet Grammar School, where he learned French; as we will see, this was to come in very handy when the lad was in his twenties. At 15, John was apprenticed to Peter Marquand, a draper in Glastonbury, some ten miles

Below
Late Victorian shopping: plenty of time to sit and relax as an order is entered into the ledger and goods are carefully weighed and beautifully wrapped.

Opposite
Had some of these finely dressed Edwardian ladies and gentlemen on their way from London's Paddington Station to the annual Regatta at Henley in 1908 chosen their fabrics and attire from John Lewis or Peter Jones? Perhaps. They certainly make a fine sight under the great roof of Brunel's station, completed in 1853, and a symbol of the Railway Age that changed the way we lived. Goods from all over the country were brought to the John Lewis store on the new railways.

west of Shepton Mallet, and, soon afterwards – Marquand died suddenly – to Joseph Tasker in a shop close to Wells Cathedral. His next port of call was with Henry Nicholls in Bridgwater who taught him that 'the art of pricing is to get profit where the public will not see it'.

By now, however, John was determined to break free of the bondage of Somerset apprenticeships and set up on his own. Sleeping under the counters of his masters' shops, as most apprentices did in those days, and being kept on a 'tight leash' by his employers cannot have been easy for an energetic young man. John left, by train, in 1855 for a short spell in Liverpool. There he worked, for £3 10s a month, for a draper named Carmichael in Church Street, one of the city's main shopping thoroughfares. Sacked for fighting, he borrowed a sovereign (a pound coin) from a fellow assistant and, in May 1856, took another train – south, to London.

This was a thrilling time to arrive in the 'Smoke'. The Great Exhibition, held in Joseph Paxton's revolutionary Crystal Palace in Hyde Park five years earlier, had shown 6 million Londoners and visitors the joys and wonders of manufactured and crafted goods shipped in from around the globe. Incomes were rising, the professional middle class was in the ascendancy and the desire to shop for fancy, exotic and luxury goods had spread – through the Aladdin's Cave-like galleries of the Crystal Palace – far beyond the landed elite. There was also talk of a proper mains sewer for London – which would help to eradicate cholera, a disease still rife in the city – and even plans for an underground railway.

Above
Joseph Paxton's Crystal Palace, housing the Great Exhibition, when brand new in 1851. The animated Hyde Park crowd wears eye-catching and even exotic dress for the occasion.

Opposite
The souks of Tunis and their teeming wares were set on either side of a wild Bedouin tent in this evidently fascinating court inside the Great Exhibition at the Crystal Palace. A taste for the exotic was being nurtured in newly affluent British shoppers.

The telephone and electric light were as yet little more than pipe dreams, yet London's West End, and especially Regent Street, shone under gas lamps late into the evenings. The latter was a glorious Regency development, fronted by the brilliant architect John Nash and brimming with seductive shops. The elegant colonnades that ran the length of this curved street were, sadly, not replaced at the time of the great rebuilding of the 1920s.

Conditions had thus been set for a retail revolution, and John Lewis was to fire one of the opening shots. For the time being, though, the young draper lodged in a Regent Street hostel with 54 other shop assistants, and was being shown the sights by his cousin Percy Godfrey. John took a job at first with Hodges & Lowman, a smallish drapery business in Regent Street, and then, at £5 a month, with Peter Robinson, whose premises were on the north-eastern corner of Oxford Circus.

For Robinson, John specialized in buying silk. This meant trips, on foot or by horse-drawn bus, to the City of London. Here, the wholesale trade, and the ships that served it from around the world through the Port of London, met the retail trade. The opulent Drapers' Hall in Throgmorton Street, last rebuilt in the late 1860s, is a reminder of the power, wealth and influence of the London drapers who have associated there since 1543.

Soon, John became Robinson's head buyer, the youngest in London. He fell in love with Eleanor Breeks, the niece of one of his wealthiest suppliers. She lived, in some style, in a house in Cumberland Terrace. This was the grandest and most romantic of the white stucco Neoclassical terraces that Nash had designed for Regent's Park, a short walk from Oxford Circus. The relationship lasted until 1875, but John was never deemed

grand enough to earn Eleanor's hand in marriage from her ambitious family. Heartbroken, he was not to marry until he was nearly 50. John was never to forget 'Nelly' Breeks, commissioning a monument in her memory after her death in 1903; she had never married.

Robinson, meanwhile, offered the young man a partnership in his business. However, by 1864 the time was ripe for John to make his own mark on the mighty, growing metropolis. With help from his unmarried sisters, who loaned him £600 from their life savings, he bought stock for 132 Oxford Street, the narrow-fronted, four-storey Georgian house that he rented on the site of today's John Lewis department store. It had been a tobacconist's and was flanked by other small businesses typical of the period: they included a bookseller, brushmaker, dentist, fruiterer, goldsmith, stay-maker (for corsets) and shoemaker.

John Lewis, whose name now fronted 132 Oxford Street, was 28 years old and brimming with energy and self-confidence. His narrow (some would say blinkered) genius lay in buying a great variety of stock, which meant that shoppers could find all they needed to clothe themselves – in an era of tailors, and decades before 'prêt-à-porter' – and selling it at a relatively low profit margin compared to his rivals. A customer whose spouse had made a packet in the drapery business told young Mr Lewis: 'You are doing what my husband did – buying cheap and selling cheap.'

The shop window was jammed with silks, laces, threads, ribbons, frills and bows. Nearly all of the goods were bought personally by John Lewis who, for the next 64 years until his death 'in harness' at the age of 92, would run his business with the proverbial rod of iron. When a well-heeled customer dared to accuse him of showing his best goods in the shop window while keeping second-rate versions behind the counter, Lewis picked him up by the collar of his coat and threw him into the street! More politely, Lewis's French came in handy as he travelled across the Channel – by paddle steamer, in those days – to run his knowing fingers through lace in Calais and silk in Lyons.

And, yet, he was not earning money anything like as quickly as the draper and shopkeeper he saw as his greatest rival. This was William Whiteley, a Yorkshireman who had come to London a year before Lewis.

Opposite
Waiting for the Queen, a lithograph celebrating the opening of the Great Exhibition by David Roberts, the famous Scottish Orientalist whose biggest fan was Queen Victoria herself. She was not amused, however, by the antics of sparrows and pigeons roosting in the trees seen here inside the Crystal Palace.

Below
After the death of Prince Albert in 1861, Queen Victoria wore black mourning clothes; here is an 1887 advert for them by Peter Robinson of Regent Street.

Below right
John Lewis worked for Peter Robinson – whose department store is seen here in 1891 – before setting up his own business in Oxford Street in 1864.

Above
New Year's portrait of a cheerless Queen
Victoria, 1890, garbed in exquisite mourning
clothes fashioned in many shades of black.

Right
One of Queen Victoria's exotic feathered
hats on show in the window of Caleys of
Windsor. The store became part of Selfridges
Provincial Stores in 1919 and was bought by
John Lewis in 1940.

AS WORN BY
HER MAJESTY QUEEN VICTORIA
SUPPLIED BY
CALEYS of WINDSOR

Whiteley created his department store from a cluster of shops on Westbourne Grove in 1867. A dab hand at self-publicity, he dubbed himself the 'Universal Provider', claiming to stock anything from a pin to an elephant. When an unwise clergyman, trying to be clever, ordered an elephant, Whiteley delivered one to his London rectory garden in double-quick time. Within 20 years, Whiteley's boasted 30 departments and a staff 6,000 strong.

Furthermore, after fire blazed through his shops in 1887, Whiteley was to commission his brand-new department-store building: a swaggering, steel-framed Edwardian Baroque shop, faced in finely carved stone. All domes and airy galleries, it was reported at the time to be an 'immense symposium of the arts and industries of the nation and of the world'. And, yet, as Lewis ploughed his narrow furrow in Oxford Street, slowly acquiring the few shops between No. 132 and Holles Street, fate caught up with the flamboyant Whiteley. In 1907, in a story given blanket coverage in the newspapers of the day, he was shot dead by a man claiming to be his illegitimate son through an alleged liaison with the sister of a Whiteley's shop assistant.

From his first day's takings of 16s 4d in 1864, John Lewis grew his business slowly and steadily. He appeared never to hurry, not least in terms of producing a potential heir to his growing, and carefully invested, fortune. In 1880, however, in Scotland on a rare holiday (like reading, playing the piano and sport, he considered holidays to be a waste of time), Mills Baker of Bristol, a fellow draper, introduced him to his younger half-sister. Somerset-born Eliza Mills was one of the first undergraduates at Girton College, Cambridge. Lewis and Miss Mills – known as Ellie – met again, by chance, two years later, on a horse-drawn bus clip-clopping along Oxford Street.

John Lewis & Company, as it was then known, Oxford Street, in 1885 when the store was still a collection of shops and houses knocked together. John Lewis's original shop was the second bay between the 'H' of John and the 'E' of Lewis.

Married in 1884, when he was 48 and she 30, they set up home together, at first in Park Square not far from the shop and where their first son, John Spedan Lewis, was born in 1885, and then in a large and gloomy Victorian house alongside Hampstead Heath. The latter had more than 1.6 hectares (4 acres) of gardens – as much as Buckingham Palace had. Here, Lewis planted durable evergreens and built a rockery from flints and pebbles picked up on East Anglian beaches and brought back to London: evidently, he did not believe in spending when there was no need to. Nor – unlike his elder son, Spedan, who was to create the John Lewis Partnership in 1929, the year after his father died – did he have time for flowers.

Dressed in frock coat and top hat, or homburg in later years, and sporting a white, spade-shaped beard, Lewis also steadfastly refused to advertise his business. There was little or no publicity. As in most stores at the time, staff wages and conditions were kept to a minimum. Young drapers' assistants coming up to make their way, if not their fortune, in London – mostly from Devon, Cornwall and Wales – were paid about £25 a year; many had to borrow to get by. The majority of Lewis' staff by the time a new, purpose-built store opened on the Oxford Street site in 1895 were young women; they lived in spartan dormitories, often two to a bed, in nearby Weymouth Street.

The situation of shop assistants generally during this period was not a happy one. They were forbidden to go out during the week. They could be fined threepence for bringing a newspaper to work, gossiping or appearing to be idle. They had to reach sales targets, and were dismissed if they dared to marry. There was no sick pay, no pensions, and with long working hours – limited to 74 a week in 1886 for staff under 18 years old – little opportunity for leisure. Despite this, staff had to keep up appearances at all times, the women and girls in high-collared black woollen dresses, shoes and stockings.

Spedan Lewis said his father knew the cost of everything; the lift for the new Oxford Street shop cost a penny-farthing each time it went up or down. Lewis could even be seen standing by the lift gates, directing shoppers he considered fit towards the stairs. His one interest beyond the business was buying property. He was, though, an honest merchant who treated his suppliers well, and was well regarded as a model, self-made Victorian businessman.

He had two sons with Ellie: John Spedan, born in 1885, and Oswald, in 1887. The boys were not baptised until their teenage years, as Lewis, a dyed-in-the-wool agnostic, thought religion 'childish'; the only creed he believed in, said Ellie, was the 'Divine Right of Employers'. And yet, despite family rows, the boys grew up in a largely happy, if extremely private, household, educated and guided by their mother. Lewis, meanwhile, commuted to Oxford Street in his horse-drawn carriage. This choice of transport was eventually replaced by a pair of Rolls-Royce Silver Ghosts, one originally fitted with a loud bell rung by Lewis to clear pedestrians from his path.

Curiously, Lewis was a Liberal, serving for many years as a councillor in both local borough and London County Council politics. However, when John Lewis staff finally took strike action in April 1920, he lashed out. Those on strike, he fired. Funds were provided to strikers by the staff of rival companies, including Harrods and the Army & Navy Stores, as well as

Whiteley's on busy Westbourne Grove shortly before the store burned down in 1887 and the later glamorous, American-style department-store buildings took its place.

by Queen Mary herself, but Lewis barked, 'If I see them on their hands and knees, I shall not take them back.' He was, as the London *Evening News* said at the time, 'fixed and unalterable'.

Dogged, and stubborn as a bulldog, Lewis had even gone to prison – three weeks in HMP Brixton – for contempt of court in 1903, in a legal wrangle over what he was allowed, or not allowed, to do with his shop, which was located on the Howard de Walden estate. For his sons, especially Spedan, all this was frustrating – not least because rival department stores were leaping ahead. In 1909, Harry Gordon Selfridge (he later dropped the name 'Harry'), a big-spirited American from the Midwest, opened the magnificent department store that bears his name on Oxford Street. So splendid was its (steel-framed) Classical design that one architect, looking at the design drawings, quipped, 'Has the Parthenon pupped?'

'Why not spend a day at Selfridges?' asked contemporary advertising. Selfridge had created a retail palace. No fewer than 80,000 people passed through its doors on its first day. They were all allowed to amble at their own pace to gawp at the goods on display between glamorous restaurants and public rooms, and the sensational sight of the aircraft that Louis Blériot had just flown across the Channel – the first pilot to do so – hanging from a stairwell.

John Lewis
– & –
Titanic Fabric

Films have yet to portray the ill-fated RMS *Titanic* in all its true Edwardian splendour. Its tragic loss on 15 April 1912, when the giant White Star liner hit an iceberg on its maiden voyage from Southampton to New York and two-thirds of its 2,224 passengers and crew perished, has long coloured its design. Third-class passengers, for example, were not nearly so badly served as Hollywood suggests, while those in First Class revelled, for those few days out from England, in surprisingly light, airy and gracious state rooms and cabins. The aim had been to create a 'floating hotel' inspired by London's Ritz Hotel, its design very different from the heavy Victorian country-house interiors of earlier transatlantic liners. A single surviving sample length of fabric (design opposite) used in the state rooms survives in the John Lewis Partnership Heritage Centre at Cookham, Berkshire. It is an exquisite, bright and cheerful Grapes and Scrolls pattern – 17 colours in all – printed on luscious chintz. It was produced exclusively for the *Titanic* and printed by Stead McAlpin at Cummersdale near Carlisle. Designed by artists in London, the blocks alone took a year to make, the entire design and production process lasting nearly two years. John Lewis owned Stead McAlpin from 1965 to 2007.

Above
Peter Jones, Sloane Square, in 1910, a year
before John Lewis bought the Star & Garter
pub – long since demolished – at the north
end of the store.

Opposite
Inside Peter Jones c.1900. The fashionable
Japanese-style parasols would have made a
light and colourful contrast to the heavy-duty
and highly polished timber display cases and
other ornate late-Victorian fittings.

John Lewis continued to run the store. Oswald took to the law and the army, while Spedan Lewis was allowed Peter Jones to run. This was the Sloane Square store that Lewis senior had bought for cash in 1906, three years after Jones himself had retired to devote himself to his art collection. John Lewis carried the lot – twenty £1,000 notes and others, totalling £22,500 – in his pocket as he walked from Oxford Street to Chelsea. It was here, in the shadow of his father, that Spedan Lewis began to put into practice the moral and commercial principles that would see Peter Jones healthily in profit. They would also lead on to the creation of that remarkable experiment in British business, the John Lewis Partnership. However, this was only possible once John Lewis himself had retired; he did so, in effect, on 8 June 1928, the day he died. Spedan stepped into his shoes, and with a spring in his step. It was as if those 50 shades of black fabric had been pinned back to let the twentieth-century sunlight shine in.

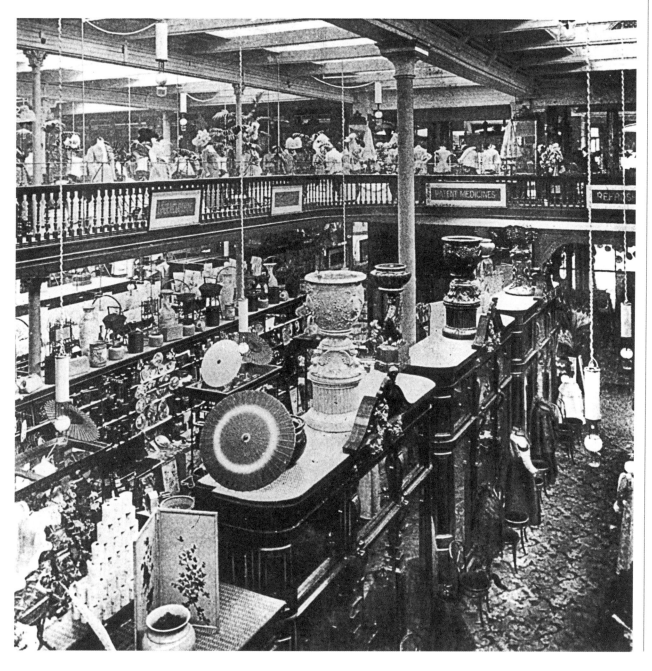

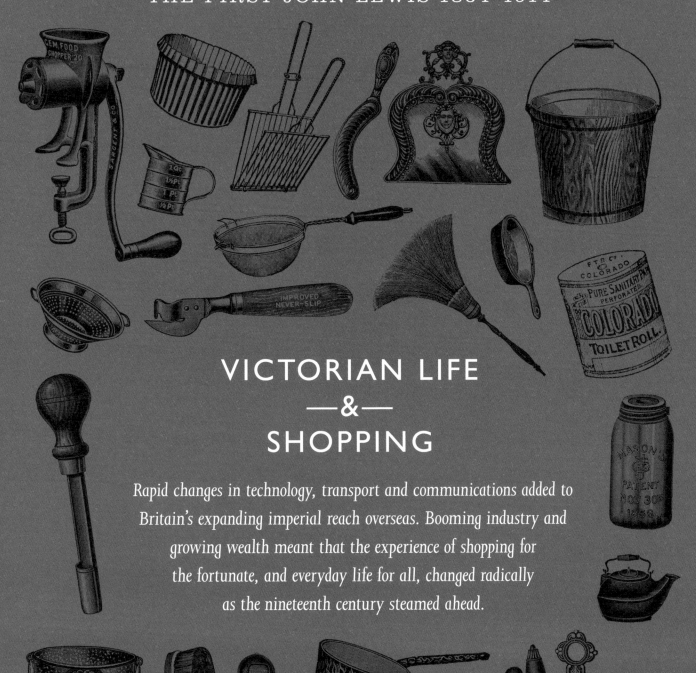

VICTORIAN LIFE
—&—
SHOPPING

Rapid changes in technology, transport and communications added to
Britain's expanding imperial reach overseas. Booming industry and
growing wealth meant that the experience of shopping for
the fortunate, and everyday life for all, changed radically
as the nineteenth century steamed ahead.

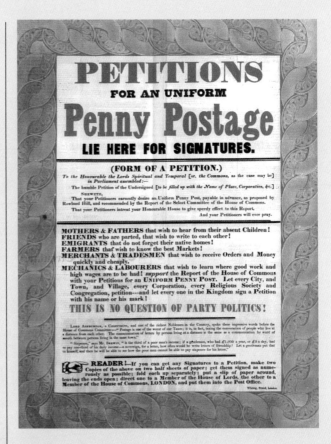

Several things happened, in a remarkable rush, to make modern shopping – and the 'brave new world' of department stores like John Lewis – possible. As Regency refinement gave way to Victorian vigour, the Industrial Revolution swept people into Britain's cities. They came, increasingly, via the steam railways, which also moved goods and food quickly and efficiently the length and breadth of the country. Soon, it was possible for fresh milk, meat and fish to be brought up to great cities like London within a few hours. This replaced the tainted, stale and sickening food to which early Victorian city dwellers had grown accustomed. The railways also brought to cities the new manufactured goods so famously showcased by the Great Exhibition of 1851 – and, as ever more of these were made, so their prices fell.

The new steamships, meanwhile, accelerated world trade. A whole host of what had, not long ago, been luxury goods – from fruit and tea to silk and raw materials – became cheaper and more freely available than ever before. The Victorians' increasing curiosity about the wider world, together with vastly improved communications, nurtured a desire for all sorts of goods, and food, that had, only a few years earlier, been the stuff of travellers' tales. The coming of the Penny Post, the electrical telegraph and, later in the century, the telephone meant increasingly rapid communication between buyers and sellers. The need for national standards, to pull this new system of communication together for the benefit of the nation, led to a spate of reforming laws passed by Parliament from the early years of Queen Victoria's reign onwards. A standard national time was agreed on. Before the coming of the railways, the time in Shepton Mallet and in Oxford Street had varied – as had the laws governing weights, measures, health and planning.

This extraordinary and seemingly relentless progress led, despite economic ups and downs, to a huge rise in population and incomes in the period between the Great

Top
The universal Penny Post marked a radical change in the pace and frequency of communications throughout Britain. This is a poster from 1839 campaigning for the service that arrived the following year.

Above
Penny Red stamp, issued from 1841 to 1879; it replaced the Penny Black of 1840 as it was easier to see the black cancellation mark (postmark) on a red background.

Opposite
Faster communications meant that fashions travelled faster, too. Here, exquisitely dressed French ladies shop for lingerie in the early 1890s in a Parisian shop. The same garments would be on sale in London almost simultaneously.

Imp. Larivière, Paris.

N° 45 — 1892
Abel Goubaud, Edr, Paris.

Exhibition of 1851 and the proclamation in 1877 of Queen Victoria as Empress of India. Imperial trade, too, gave a huge boost to the British economy. It also brought yet more enticing, exotic goods to a new generation of shops – especially to the first department stores, John Lewis's Oxford Street flagship among them. Between 1861 and 1901, the population of England and Wales grew from 20 million to 32.5 million, while incomes rose 40 per cent between 1880 and 1900 alone, in an age of low inflation.

Much of Britain's increasing wealth was generated by its rising and ambitious middle classes. Through a series of electoral reform acts from 1832 onwards, they were given the vote, their status in society was raised and their value was recognized. The rise of the professional middle classes, and the many clerks and secretaries who worked for them, also led to a prolonged housing boom, which in turn meant an ever greater need for furnishings, fabrics and, increasingly, luxuries. Furniture shops, drapers and, then, department stores all benefited from the unstoppable rise of the British middle class.

Initially, this boom led to a spate of often hideous, overblown design and decoration by the newly rich. Yet, increasingly, and especially as women came out of the shadows, there was a demand for 'artistic' goods and furnishings. In a lecture given in 1880 to the Birmingham Society of Arts and School of Design, William Morris – craftsman, textile designer, socialist and writer – told a spellbound audience: 'Have nothing in your houses that you do not know to be useful, or believe to be beautiful.' The clutter of mid-Victorian homes gave way in refined and educated circles to an aesthetic grace, and the department

Regent Street at its imperial peak in the late 1890s, before it was completely rebuilt.

Opposite
William Morris fabrics set the tone for the interiors of cultured middle-class British homes as the Arts and Crafts movement gathered pace from the 1860s.

Right
A Morris adjustable chair, designed by the architect Philip Webb, its wooden frame upholstered in a hand-woven William Morris bird fabric.

Right below
Philip Webb also designed this remarkably light and fashion-setting, timber country-style 'Sussex' chair for Morris & Co.

stores that emerged at much the same time as Morris's lecture were willing and able to meet this new demand.

However, the actual experience of Victorian shopping – whether for high-quality food or well-designed goods – was slow to change until the arrival in London of John Lewis and his fellow drapers. Even then, shoppers were not encouraged to linger. As soon as they walked into these large stores, they were met by shopwalkers, men in formal dress who ran their departments with military precision: nothing escaped their beady eyes – least of all, customers. A shopper was led, almost by the nose, to counters where rolls of fabrics or other goods were fetched by poorly paid assistants, many of whom worked 90 hours a week.

Once a purchase had been agreed, the bill was signed with a flourish by the shopwalker, who would then escort the shopper from the premises. It was not, in fact, until Gordon Selfridge opened his spectacular department store on Oxford Street, between John Lewis and Marble Arch, that shoppers were allowed to wander around unguided, with assistants on call to help when needed. It was at this moment that shopping became fun, a form of leisure and simple lollygagging (how John Lewis must have disapproved!) rather than a formal exchange of money for goods between buyer and seller.

It was the American-born Selfridge, more even than William Whiteley, who made retailing a part of London's social whirl – glamorous, and even risqué. 'People will sit up and take notice of you if you will sit up and take notice of what makes them sit up and take notice', said Selfridge. The British public certainly took notice of Selfridge's own behaviour when, after the death of his wife, he took up scandalously with one – and possibly both – of the Dolly Sisters, a pair of racy Hungarian-born, convent-educated vaudeville stars. Selfridge blew a great deal of his immense Oxford Street fortune on Jenny and Rosie. He bankrolled their enormous gambling debts, flew ice cream from London to Paris for them, and even sent

VICTORIAN HATS

1860s
A jaunty fur hat designed by the
long-lived Parisian milliner and fashion designer
Caroline Reboux, who had shops in Paris and London,
and went on to style hats for Marlene Dietrich
and the Duchess of Windsor.

1865
A civilian version of the Glengarry bonnet,
a form of headgear worn by Scottish regiments
of the British army. Queen Victoria was, of
course, fond of Scotland. Velvet over metal,
with ribbon and feather trim.

1870
Pretty, low-crowned French straw hat by the milliner
Pascal Amarante. Edged in black velvet, it is adorned
with black velvet asterisks and a black silk satin ribbon,
and festooned with artificial ears of wheat, ferny fronds,
pink roses and a purple iris fashioned from feathers.

1885
Extravagant, high-crowned brown felt Parisian hat, for
making an entrance, with a narrow rim decorated with
painted wooden beads. A feather and painted wood
bird is ensnared in a festoon of chenille and silk ribbons.

1870s

A high-crowned and well-rounded wedding bonnet that might have doubled as a festive solar topee for travel 'out East'. Fashioned in ivory satin – although this example was originally pale blue – and trimmed with silk ribbons set off with artificial white lilac and tinted velvet ivy leaves.

1870s

A happy English girl's straw boater that calls to mind Victorian seaside holidays and decorous strolls in polite city parks. With its sensible and stylish wide brim, this one has a band and a big, floppy bow made of blue silk ribbon. A style that endured until World War I.

1898

A decidedly cocky split-straw 'pork pie' hat, made in Britain for sale in the US. The band is black satin decorated with a black and white feather cockade. The hat is lined in white rayon, a man-made material imitating silk, wool, cotton and linen that went into commercial production in 1891.

1900

One for Cowes Week, perhaps, or the Henley Royal Regatta, but certainly not one for Admirals of the Queen's navy. A bicorne hat, made in England, covered in silk and satin set off by strings of steel beads.

An elegant London lady sets off for a social visit, and perhaps a shopping spree, too. A hansom cab is seen overtaking behind the top-hatted businessman. *The Bayswater Omnibus* by George William Joy, 1895.

them a pair of tortoises with 4-carat blue Cartier diamonds set into their shells; the girls took them for strolls along the seafront at Le Touquet.

Selfridge thus shocked a public hungry for tittle-tattle and scandal. But he believed, in his time-honoured phrase that 'the customer is always right', and made retailing as newsworthy and as sensational as the new-fangled flying machines, turbine-driven transatlantic liners and world speed records. He also lost his business through reckless spending. John Lewis, who had little time for fun or leisure – let alone for excess and scandal – carried on trading; he may have lacked the flamboyance of Selfridge or Whiteley, but his business prospered steadily.

Nonetheless, both Selfridge, who died in a two-bedroom flat in Putney, and William Whiteley, shot dead in the office of his department store on Westbourne Grove, enjoyed an understanding of another Victorian phenomenon that was to grow beyond all measure in the twentieth century: mass media. The reduction by Parliament of costly stamp duty on newspapers in 1836, the year John Lewis was born, saw circulations soar. That year, 39 million newspapers were sold in England, increasing to 122 million in 1854. New papers aimed at the rising middle class – notably the *Daily Telegraph*, founded in 1855 – were immensely successful and highly influential.

The *Telegraph*'s editor, Thornton Leigh Hunt, a Liberal, noted in a memorandum penned that year:

'We should report all striking events in science, so told that the intelligent public can understand what has happened and can see its bearing on our daily life and our future. The same principle should apply to all other events – to fashion, to new inventions, to new methods of conducting business.'

It is fascinating to see 'fashion' in the list of subjects that Leigh Hunt deemed important in the mid-1850s. He was certainly right, however: by 1890, his paper could boast the world's largest circulation.

In 1896, a brash newcomer arrived in Fleet Street, the *Daily Mail*, aimed head-on at the lower middle classes, those ranks of suburban commuters who were by now an all-important part of the story of British retailing. The *Mail* sold a million copies a day. John Lewis was flatly opposed to advertising, sales gimmicks and media exposure. But his rivals quickly established a mutually beneficial relationship with mass-market newspapers and with the growing number of magazines devoted to the home, its furnishing and decor. The rise of the mass media coincided with another new development that Lewis had taken against: the branch shop. The Home and Colonial chain of food shops founded by Julius Drewe in 1883, with a small grocery shop on London's Edgware Road, flourished along with the *Daily Mail*. By the end of the century, it boasted 100 branches – and it had over 3,000 by the time John Lewis died in 1928.

This luxurious, colour-coordinated bedroom – pink and gold – is from a late-Victorian catalogue from Heelas of Reading, a shop bought into the John Lewis fold in the twentieth century.

Victorian ladies' fashion was never less than extravagant, demanding and even a little daunting. From left to right: hoop skirt from 1864, bustle dress of 1870, balloon sleeves for 1880, and 1900s wasp waist.

This once-famous grocery chain vanished years ago into the Safeway empire. Nonetheless, it is a reminder of how dynamic Victorian entrepreneurs – taking full advantage of new forms of communication, international trade, free markets and mass media – could build hugely powerful trading empires within just a few years. Drewe, who began his career as a tea buyer in China in the 1870s, became so wealthy that he even built a brand-new granite castle in Devon, Castle Drogo.

John Lewis had been born into an earlier, and very different, era and background from that of flamboyant figures like Selfridge and Drewe. He was cautious rather than cavalier in his approach to life and business. Above

all, and no matter what one can put down to inherent character traits, Lewis was a man from an old-fashioned and rather puritanical English market town, a young fellow from a long-established trade and with old-fashioned skill in his fingers. Small wonder, then, that he was never able or willing to make his Oxford Street shop into the kind of popular pleasure palaces that Whiteley and Selfridge shaped in London; in short, he was not a 'modern Victorian'.

And yet, even John Lewis had to bend with the times. His new shop, opened in 1895 and replacing the existing Georgian houses on the Oxford Street site, boasted a public restaurant as well as staff dining rooms. Shops had become places to enjoy, to spend time in and to think about purchases rather than simply spaces where money was handed over for goods that customers already knew they needed. Who would want to eat in a shop? John Lewis must have thought before agreeing to a restaurant. And yet, people did – especially women.

The role of women marked one of the great changes in nineteenth-century shopping, as it evolved from the era of the Great Exhibition in Hyde Park to grand department stores half a century on. In the preceding century and until the Regency era, shopping had been more a male than a female pursuit. Indeed, this remains true of traditional societies around the world in the twenty-first century. The reasons are not hard to see, either then or now. It was not simply that a woman's place was in the home, but that city streets were often unsafe for them to wander through alone. They depended on men for money, and, in any case, most shops were rather basic – little more than warehouses with a nameboard attached or a sign hanging from their street fronts.

The rise of increasingly comfortable shops, with gas and then electric lighting – and, in particular, those with female staff – changed this situation radically. Shops were now safe places for women to go and to meet friends and relatives – and where they might have met to discuss their plans for emancipation. When retailers began offering restaurants, too, with toilets and cloakrooms, this was a further encouragement for women to get out and about, and it meant that they could stay out of the home for longer. Pubs, clubs and dining rooms were almost exclusively the preserve of men, and often smoky and drunken with it. Throughout the second half of the nineteenth century, it is possible to trace the growing feminine influence on shops and shopping, from the design, layout, decor and facilities to the goods offered and the way in which they were sold. Most women preferred to buy from female assistants,

A woman's place had been in the home until the advent of safely lit and policed Victorian streets and of the department store itself. Women's liberation was around the corner from this 1899 oil by Alexander Rossi, *News from the Front*, painted during the Boer War.

Shops as far as the Victorian eye can see: New Oxford Street, with shops now stretching from here all the way to Marble Arch to the west in one long unbroken line.

SANDERS & SONS

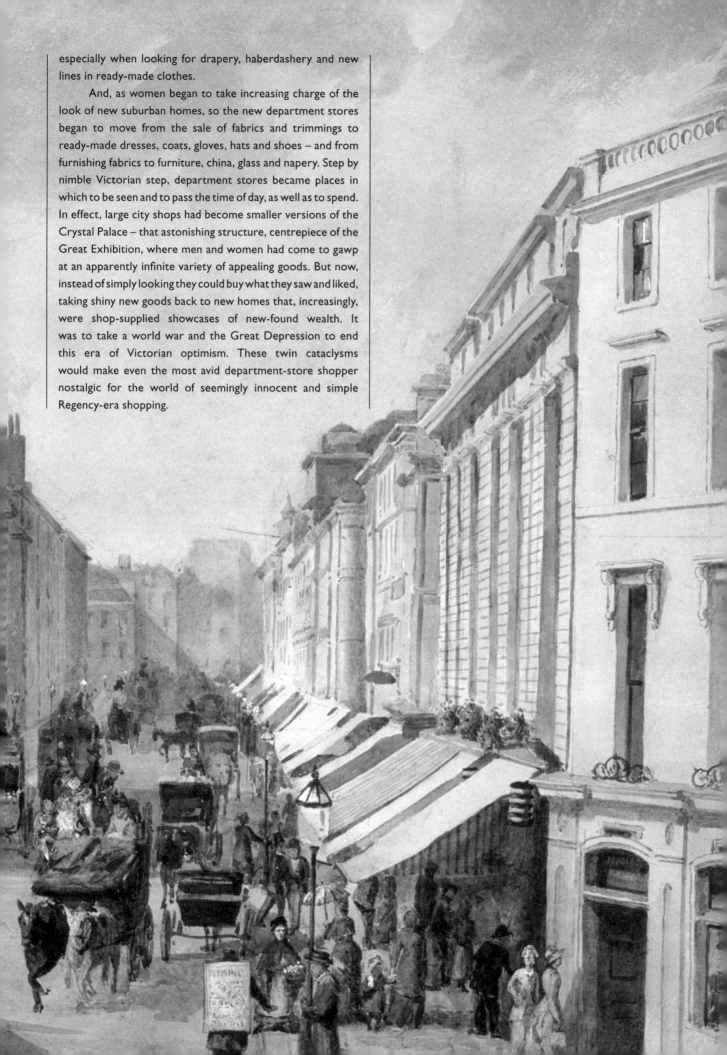

especially when looking for drapery, haberdashery and new lines in ready-made clothes.

And, as women began to take increasing charge of the look of new suburban homes, so the new department stores began to move from the sale of fabrics and trimmings to ready-made dresses, coats, gloves, hats and shoes – and from furnishing fabrics to furniture, china, glass and napery. Step by nimble Victorian step, department stores became places in which to be seen and to pass the time of day, as well as to spend. In effect, large city shops had become smaller versions of the Crystal Palace – that astonishing structure, centrepiece of the Great Exhibition, where men and women had come to gawp at an apparently infinite variety of appealing goods. But now, instead of simply looking they could buy what they saw and liked, taking shiny new goods back to new homes that, increasingly, were shop-supplied showcases of new-found wealth. It was to take a world war and the Great Depression to end this era of Victorian optimism. These twin cataclysms would make even the most avid department-store shopper nostalgic for the world of seemingly innocent and simple Regency-era shopping.

A MODEL PARTNERSHIP

1914–39

The establishment of the John Lewis Partnership was a revolution in the way a company could be structured, owned and run. John Spedan Lewis suggested various ways in which the idea occurred to him. Sometimes he claimed that it came to him in a 'Eureka!' moment in the bath. At other times, the inspiration had apparently struck him as the London General horse bus he was travelling on one day in 1907 turned the corner from Haymarket into Trafalgar Square.

It seems more likely, if less dramatic, that the idea of constituting a company so that it was owned by all those who worked for it had been nurtured over a number of years. There was a period, between 1909 and 1911, and before he became prodigiously busy, when Spedan Lewis had plenty of time to think about the future. He was 24 years old, and working for his father in the Oxford Street store, when he was thrown from his horse in Regent's Park while riding from his home in Hampstead. After painful bouts of pleurisy and emphysema, Spedan underwent two operations and lost a lung. He had very nearly died, and was forced to take a long time off work. Understandably, he was to remain something of a hypochondriac for the rest of his life.

Spedan bought a 25-hectare (63-acre) farm in Harrow – reached easily by train from central London – and here he rested while he healed. A business, he began to think, was not simply a machine for making money, but rather a 'living thing with rights of its own'. Moreover,

> its earnings should be used exactly as a good farmer feels a duty to maintain
> and develop the fertility of the land that he farms and to leave it in better
> rather than worse health than when it came into his hands.

More than this, there was something wrong in managers and principals earning so much money from the labour of others. They should earn what lawyers, architects or doctors made at the time, Spedan said, while a company should distribute its non-voting shares to employees, who would be free to keep or sell them. Warming to his theme over the next few years, and especially during World War I, Spedan began to plan

Opposite
A smartly dressed middle-class housewife inspects her new 1935-model Wilsons & Mathiesons gas cooker.

Above
John Spedan Lewis in 1906, the year this 21-year-old business pioneer joined the firm as director of Peter Jones.

a 'far-reaching experiment in industrial democracy' designed to 'limit the earnings of capital and divide the rest among the workers'. Management should be accountable to employees, while the 'days when a lot of shareholders could stay at home and take a very large proportion of the earnings of a business' would be well and truly over.

The logical conclusion of Spedan's thinking was the creation of a business partnership through which there would be a 'sharing of gain, sharing of knowledge and sharing of power'. Increasingly messianic in his tone, he went on to proclaim: 'Partnership is justice. Better than justice, it is kindness.' What he was proposing, and what he put into practice just before the Wall Street Crash in 1929, was not just radical, but revolutionary. Here was a wealthy man who, after the death of his father, stood to gain complete ownership and control of the family business, planning a new model of commercial enterprise and one that, ultimately, would exclude its creator from power.

Lewis later wrote of that mythical London bus ride:

I can vividly remember the warm glow that ran through me as for a moment I saw something of the satisfaction of those who renounce — and afterwards do not regret renouncing — great wealth and choose a life of extreme material simplicity.

Although Spedan Lewis was in many ways an 'original', these thoughts — remarkable and unexpected for a young man in his position — were to some extent shaped by powerful currents of contemporary political thought. These had, in 1906, swept a dynamic and reformist Liberal Party into power at Westminster with a majority of 125 seats. Along with them came the first 29 Labour MPs. New ideas — socialist as well as liberal, and Marxist — had been brewing in the minds of philosophers, political activists and even designers and shopkeepers like William Morris, a founding member of the increasingly radical Socialist League in 1884.

Significantly, when, in 1906, those first Labour MPs were asked what book had most affected them, the answer was not *The Communist Manifesto* or even the Bible, but *Unto This Last* (1859) by John Ruskin. Born in 1819, the son of a successful wine and sherry merchant, Ruskin inherited a fortune when he turned 21. By the time of his death in 1900, he had given virtually every last penny away on good causes; his books on art, architecture and political economy earned him enough to live comfortably.

With biblical high-mindedness and coruscating wit, Ruskin, who, unselfconsciously, had assumed the role of Britain's national archangel, tore apart the workings of the Victorian political economy and all its divisions of wealth and countless injustices. Ultimately, said Ruskin,

There is no wealth but life. Life, including all its powers of love, of joy, and of admiration. That country is the richest which nourishes the greatest number of noble and happy human beings; that man is richest who, having perfected the functions of his own life, to the utmost, has also the widest helpful influence, both personal, and by means of his possessions, over the lives of others.

Top
Craftsman, social reformer and revolutionary: William Morris photographed by Frederick Hollyer in 1884.

Above
John Ruskin, the great Victorian critic and radical thinker, photographed here in 1870, was a huge influence on social reformers, Liberal, Tory and Labour, from the 1860s to World War I.

Had Spedan Lewis read Ruskin? It seems likely, as Ruskin's books sold in tens of thousands and his message was one that encouraged the founding of the welfare state after World War II. Spedan may also have been influenced by the model of New Lanark in Scotland, set up by the philanthropist mill owner Robert Owen, with its social and welfare programmes and improved conditions for the mill workers.

Spedan Lewis made it clear that his reasons for creating the John Lewis Partnership were nothing to do with religious belief. And yet, he had been disturbed, when his father brought him into the business in 1906 with a quarter share of the company valued at £50,000, that the family earned £26,000 that year while the 300 staff made just £16,000 between them – and only four of these earned more than £5 a week. Shopwalkers made £100, while a buyer with five years' experience might expect up to £150. Spedan found it wrong that his father should spend so much on buying property, and on litigation, while paying his staff so little and failing to plough profits back into the business. He felt that the Oxford Street store was inefficiently used and that, overall, it was 'no more than a second-rate success achieved in a first-rate opportunity'. His father would hear none of this, and carried on regardless.

Spedan's opportunity to work out his own methods of doing business and running a company came in 1914 when his father appointed him chairman of Peter Jones, the Chelsea department store he had bought for cash in 1906 and that had seemed incapable of turning a profit, much less paying a dividend. Aside from giving Spedan the opportunity to prove himself, the appointment also got him out of his father's hair, although not completely. In fact, John Lewis insisted that Spedan work a full day at the Oxford Street store; only from 5pm was he allowed to head down to the King's Road.

This intensely hard-working young man, nicknamed Speedy as a child, was eager to get hold of his father's business. As a boy, Spedan had been in awe of his father, thinking of him as a 'superman, virtually infallible in matters of business'. Spedan himself was to be thought of in similar fashion, especially in the early years of the Partnership.

A serious child who, a contemporary recalled, was 'very impressive and monumental . . . a tall, bony figure with a rather dictatorial manner', Spedan grew up to be an imposing young man. He was handsome, impeccably dressed, beautifully mannered, a good talker – many colleagues said he liked the sound of his own voice – and comfortable in the company of women. He was also famously quick-tempered and, like his father, an autocratic and domineering figure in many ways – although, as was often noted, Spedan was also all but classless. He had no interest in social hierarchy, social climbing or 'who's who'. Most of all, he valued intelligent, hard-working people of whatever background.

With his father's wealth and his mother's warmth Spedan enjoyed a privileged childhood. A Queen's Scholar at Westminster School, Spedan enjoyed tennis, cricket, hockey, skiing, debating, boxing and chess. He also developed a passion for wildlife and natural history, and became a keen amateur botanist and ornithologist. He was a member of the Zoological Society of London and its Vice President in the 1930s.

However, before he could create his own way of life, Spedan had to prove to his formidable father what he was capable of. And the results in his first few years at Peter Jones were promising. There was certainly much to do, as the Chelsea store had fallen into neglect in the years leading up to World War I. After his riding accident and subsequent illness, Spedan had been officially categorized C3, physically, which meant that he was not called up in the war. His younger brother, Oswald, went off to fight with the Westminster Dragoons, but in 1915 fell from his horse while on duty in Egypt and was packed off home with a damaged hip; he was discharged in 1916. Unlike Spedan, he was never keen to make a career in business. Relinquishing all interests to his brother in 1926, Oswald went on to serve as Conservative MP for Colchester for many years, keeping stolidly to the back benches. He returned to the John Lewis fold in 1951 as Director of Financial Operations, retiring in 1963.

By 1914, Peter Jones had become rather shabby, and, indeed, the top end of the King's Road was a curious mix of the genteel and the downright scruffy. The only part of the enterprise to make money was the Star & Garter, a pub on the corner of Sloane Square that formed a part of the Peter Jones enclave. It had been sold to John Lewis with an unexpected treasure in its cellars, 180 litres (40 gallons) of 1875 Martell brandy.

Aside from giving the shop a thorough spring clean, Spedan instigated a number of far-reaching reforms almost as soon as he first walked through the door of Peter Jones as the store's chairman. The working day was shortened by an hour. Wages were raised, and paid weekly rather than every four weeks as they had been in the past, and fairer commissions were paid on sales. Morning coffee and afternoon tea breaks were introduced. Catering was improved. Annual leave was increased to three weeks. Staff accommodation at the back of the shop was equipped with bathrooms and hot and cold running water. Those aged over 21 were free to come and go as they pleased, although the company continued to act as virtual parents for younger employees – especially those John Lewis continued to refer to as 'maidens'. Practices that were to form the basis of the Partnership principles were put in place. Staff committees were established with elected representatives; the first Committee for Communications was established in 1915 and the first Staff Council in 1919. Recreation was on offer on the playing fields that Spedan had established around his farm at Harrow.

Staff morale improved considerably, while new staff included smart, well-bred and well-educated young men and women easily able to deal on a level with grand customers from neighbouring Belgravia. In 1918 Spedan launched a staff journal, *The Gazette*, which he used as a vehicle for his latest ideas as well as a forum for views from all staff, who were encouraged to say exactly what they thought. It is still going strong and very much a part of John Lewis today. Naturally, many were suspicious, and yet throughout his time with Peter Jones and the John Lewis Partnership, Spedan held no grudges against members of staff who dared to stand up to him in print. Letters could be sent and printed anonymously, and still are today. However, sitting at the editors' sides and reading proofs of *The Gazette* with an eagle eye, he allowed himself

THE GAZETTE

OF PETER JONES, LIMITED.
SLOANE SQUARE, LONDON, S.W.3.

FOR THE PUBLICATION OF FACTS, OPINIONS AND IDEAS OF INTEREST TO
ANY ONE WHOSE FORTUNES ARE FOR THE TIME CONNECTED IN SOME
DEGREE WITH THOSE OF THE COMPANY.

SATURDAY, MARCH 16TH, 1918.

Our Policy, Rules of Correspondence, etc., are on the last page of this issue.

NOTICE FROM THE MANAGEMENT TO THE COMPANY'S STAFF.

Official Communications to this Paper are equivalent to House Notices, and must be
known by every one whom they concern.

TO MY FELLOW-EMPLOYEES OF PETER JONES, LTD.

LADIES AND GENTLEMEN,

The main purpose of this paper you will see in a general way from the paragraphs on the last page, which are intended to appear always, or at least frequently. But I think it may be useful if in this first issue I try to put my ideas with regard to it more fully before you than can be done there.

There can be no doubt that large-scale industry has come to stay. Whatever may be the ultimate economic cause or causes, it is certain that in our own, as in many other occupations, men and women achieve their purpose better, that is to say they get a greater result for any given amount of effort, by working in large teams than by working in small ones. We cannot help seeing that the big factory can produce exactly the same thing cheaper than can the little factory, and that the big shop can likewise beat its little rivals by offering the public greater variety or better value or a combination of both. Some people argue that cheapness is not everything, and that the world might contain more happiness if goods were dearer but more men and women worked " on their own account." I think these people are wrong. I think they fail to see that cheapness is really human liberty : that, if everything were to be had absolutely free of charge, every one would be absolutely free, so long, of course, as the law restrained mere bodily strength as it does now ; and that, this being so, cheapness is in itself wholly good and desirable.

Look at it like this :

Suppose 1,000 men, in order to support themselves and their families, have to make 1,000 wardrobes every year. Suppose that each man working by himself must be at work sixteen hours a day, seven days a week all the year through, to finish his one wardrobe. Is that man really free, although he is working in his own home and on his own account ? Is it freedom to be obliged, on pain of starvation, to work sixteen hours every day of the year ?

Now, suppose that those 1,000 men combine into one team and become each of them a specialist in one or two of all the different jobs that go to the making of a wardrobe, and use in one factory such machinery as cannot

Left
First edition of *The Gazette*, for the staff of Peter Jones, fronted with an editorial by Spedan Lewis, 16 March 1918.

Opposite
Then as now, Peter Jones offered women a wide range of clothes, everything from everyday underwear to bedroom robes.

very full rights of reply. A fluent and highly articulate speaker, he was a prolific writer.

Although Peter Jones did make profits in some years, this was a particularly difficult time for the retail trade. By the end of the war, the shop was in urgent need of working capital. Refusing to let his staff down, Spedan sold his Harrow farm and playing fields, and moved into a flat. There were times, however, when he thought that perhaps he should give it all up and settle for an untroubled life as a wandering naturalist.

Nonetheless, what Spedan had bought was the loyalty of his staff. His father had made no improvements to staff conditions and welfare at Oxford Street, and so he was taken aback when, in 1920, John Lewis staff went on strike – for the first and only time – for five long weeks. Even so, trade at Oxford Street was lucrative and Lewis had to bail out his son's Peter

PETER JONES LTD

No. 74.

No. 75.

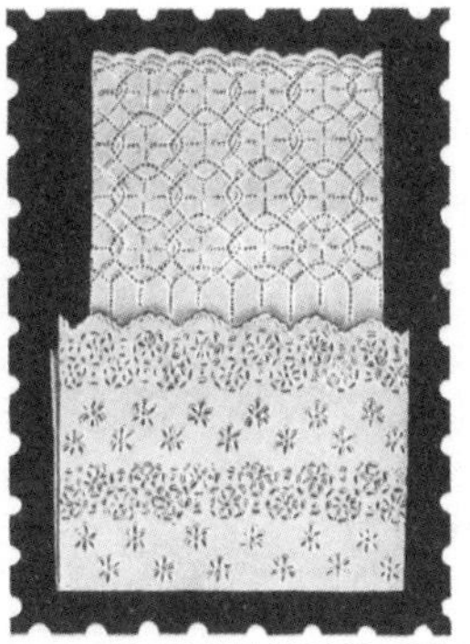

No. 74. FINE CAMBRIC EMBROIDERY. 16in. per yard 2/3½
26½in. CAMI-KNICKER FLOUNCING. Post free. per yard 3/11

No. 75. DAINTY CAMBRIC EMBROIDERY.

	Price, post free, Yard.	Doz. Yds.
1in. Insertion	4¾d.	4/8
1¼in. ,, ...	7¾d.	7/8
2in. ,, ...	9¾d.	9/8
2¼in. Edging	4¾d.	4/8
3½in. ,, ...	7¾d.	7/8
4in. ,, ...	8¾d.	8/6
5½in. ,, ...	11¾d.	11/8
8in. ,, ...	1/3½	15/3
16½in. ,, ...	2/3½	—
25in. ,, ...	2/11½	—
42in. ,, ...	5/6	—
21in. Allover	4/6	—

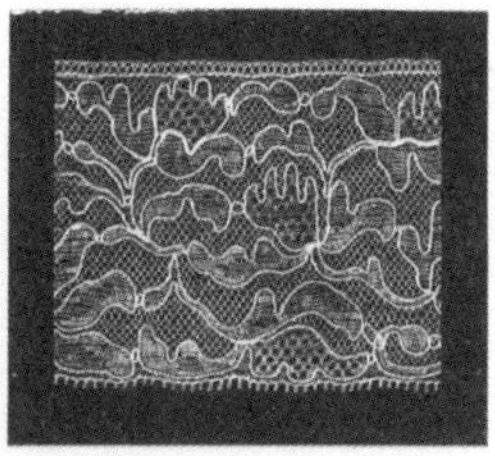

No. 77. IMITATION MALINES LACE AND INSERTION, real lace colour.

	Price per yd.	dozen. yds.
2¼in. Waved Insertion ..	10¼d.	10/8
1¼in. Edging	5¾d.	5/8
2¾in. ,, ...	11¾d.	11/8
5½in. ,, ...	1/9½	21/-
8¾in. ,, ...	2/6½	—
11in. ,, ...	3/11	—
17in. ,, ...	5/11	—
38in. Allover	10/11	—
4½in. Vandyck	1/3½	15/3
7¼in. ,, ...	1/11½	—

No. 76. IMITATION VALENCIENNES LACE AND INSERTION, real lace colour.

	Price, post free. Yard.	Doz. yds.
⅞in. Insertion	5¾d.	5/8
1¼in. ,, ...	7¾d.	7/8
2½in. Waved	1/3½	15/3
¾in. Edging	5¾d.	5/8
1¾in. ,, ...	10¾d.	10/8
2½in. ,, ...	1/3½	15/3
4¼in. ,, ...	1/9½	21/-

No. 78.

No. 79.

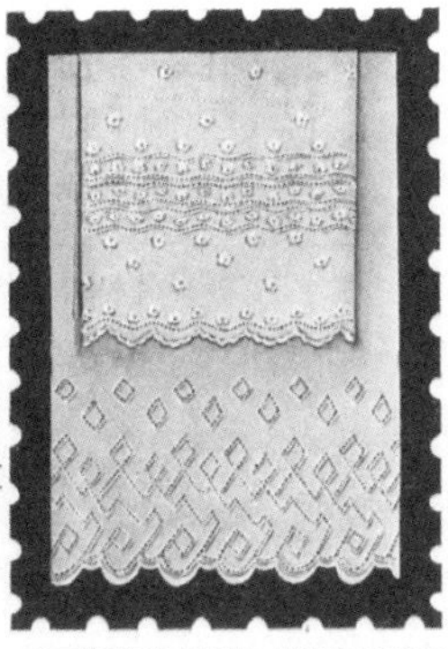

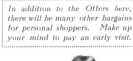

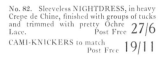

No. 78. FINE CAMBRIC EMBROIDERY.

	Yard.	Doz. Yds.
½-in. Insertion	3¾d.	3/8
¾-in. ,, ...	6¾d.	6/8
1in. ,, ...	7¾d.	7/8
1¼in. Edging	4¾d.	4/8
1¾in. ,, ...	6¾d.	6/8
3½in. ,, ...	11¾d.	11/8
5in. ,, ...	1/3½	15/3
12in. ,, ...	1/11½	—
16in. ,, ...	2/4½	—
24in. ,, ...	3/6	—
1½in. Frilled	9¾d.	9/8
2½in. ,, ...	1/3½	15/3
4in. ,, ...	1/9½	—

No. 79. FINE CAMBRIC EMBROIDERY. 16in. per yard 2/3½
26½in. CAMI-KNICKER FLOUNCING. per yard 3/11

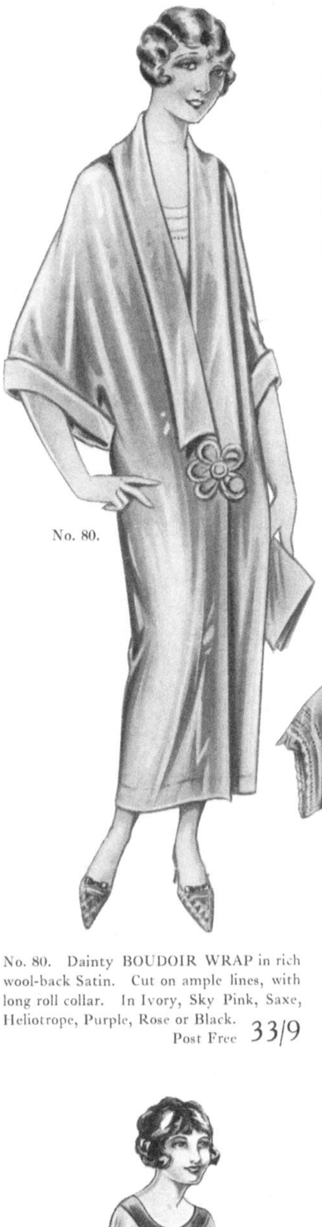

No. 80.

No. 80. Dainty BOUDOIR WRAP in rich wool-back Satin. Cut on ample lines, with long roll collar. In Ivory, Sky Pink, Saxe, Heliotrope, Purple, Rose or Black. Post Free 33/9

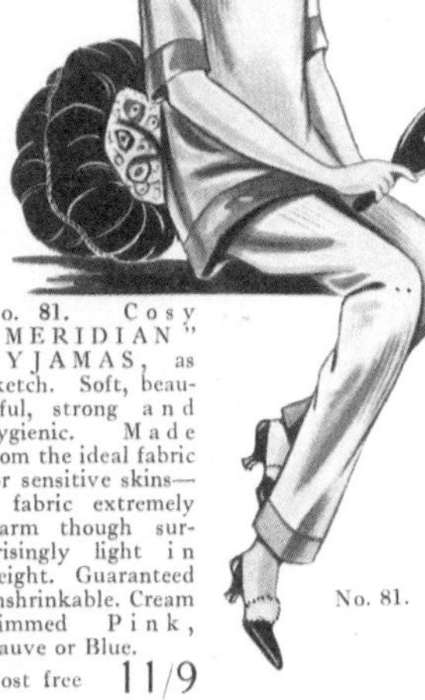

No. 81.

No. 81. Cosy "MERIDIAN" PYJAMAS, as sketch. Soft, beautiful, strong and hygienic. Made from the ideal fabric for sensitive skins—a fabric extremely warm though surprisingly light in weight. Guaranteed unshrinkable. Cream trimmed Pink, Mauve or Blue.

Post free 11/9

No. 82. Sleeveless NIGHTDRESS, in heavy Crepe de Chine, finished with groups of tucks and trimmed with pretty Ochre Lace. Post Free 27/6

CAMI-KNICKERS to match Post Free 19/11

No. 83. French Embroidered Cambric NIGHTDRESSES, with scalloping at neck and sleeves. Post Free 6/11

KNICKERS to match Post Free 3/11

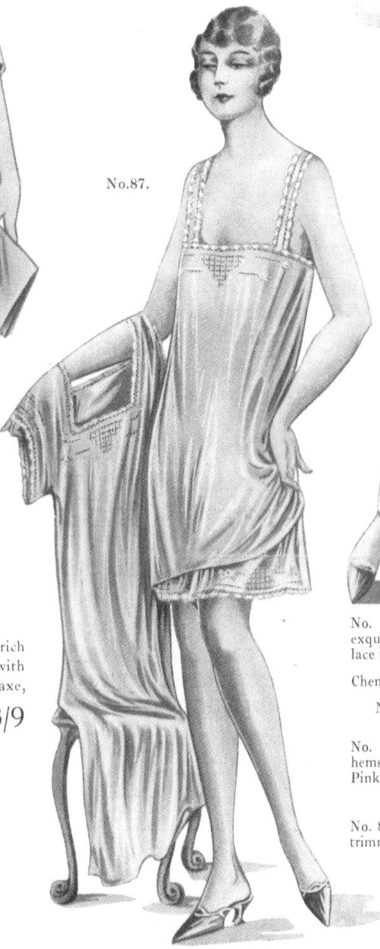

No.87.

No. 87. Dainty Set of FINE LAWN LINGERIE, with Val. Lace trimming and Hand-Drawn thread work. Price, Post Free.

Chemise 6/11 Knickers 6/11

Nightdresses 13/11

No. 88. "MERIDIAN" Nightdresses, magyar shape, bound neck. Made of same soft, strong, warm texture as "Meridian" Pyjamas and bound neck and sleeves with Pink, Mauve or Blue. Post Free 12/11

Similar Nightdresses with square necks, lace trimmed. Post Free 16/11

No. 89. "MERIDIAN" Unshrinkable COMBINATIONS, very soft and durable texture, non-irritating to the most sensitive skins. Sleeveless, low neck, trimmed lace, as sketch, or with short sleeves and low or V necks. O.S. 1/- extra. Post Free 9/11

No. 90. Fine Silk and Wool COMBINATIONS, opera shape, inserted lace border at top. In Pink and White. O.S. 19/6. Post Free 18/6

No. 91. Spun Silk COMBINATIONS. Delightful for evening wear. Lace inlet at top. Opera shape. Post Free 25/9

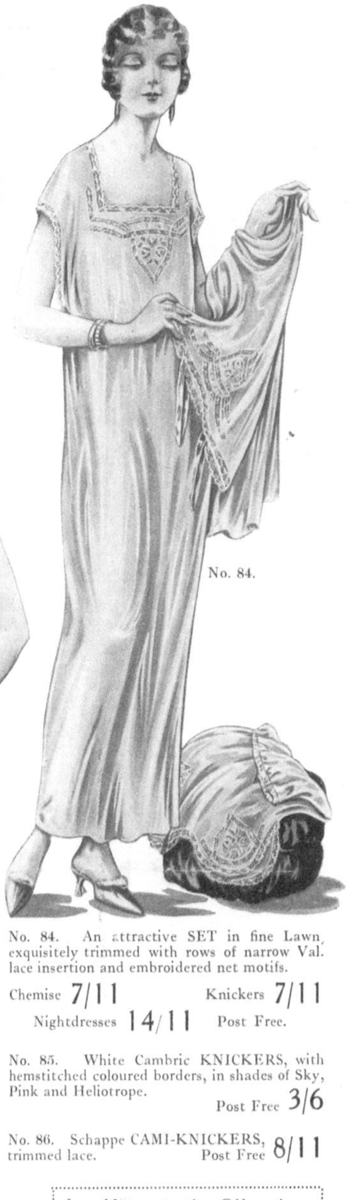

No. 84.

No. 84. An attractive SET in fine Lawn, exquisitely trimmed with rows of narrow Val. lace insertion and embroidered net motifs.

Chemise 7/11 Knickers 7/11

Nightdresses 14/11 Post Free.

No. 85. White Cambric KNICKERS, with hemstitched coloured borders, in shades of Sky, Pink and Heliotrope. Post Free 3/6

No. 86. Schappe CAMI-KNICKERS, trimmed lace. Post Free 8/11

In addition to the Offers here, there will be many other bargains for personal shoppers. Make up your mind to pay an early visit.

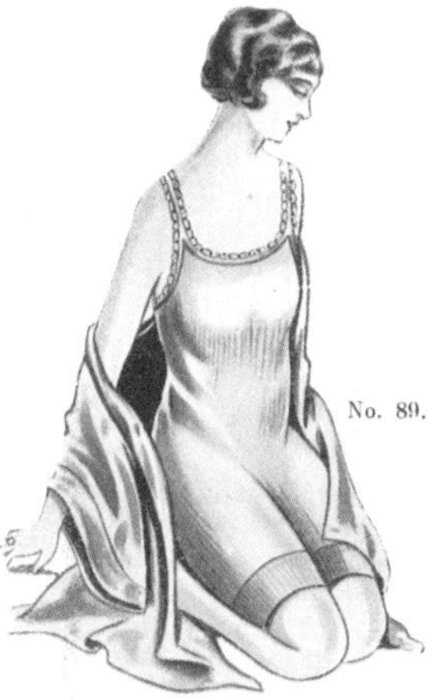

No. 89.

THE BEST VALUE IN LONDON

JOHN LEWIS ON STRIKE

When John Lewis staff went on strike on 27 April 1920, their fate was sealed. John Lewis made it crystal clear that he would not take them back even if they 'came crawling on hands and knees'. The 400 strikers might have gained public sympathy, but Lewis referred to 'accursed trade unionists' and refused to allow his staff the right of free association that, by 1920, had been accepted by most British industrialists and entrepreneurs.

The strike had been about union recognition. Lewis stood his ground. When the strike was called for the day of a big John Lewis sale, with a vast stock of surplus government silk to be sold cheaply, he closed every other department and had his loyal 100 'blacklegs' do a roaring trade, selling the entire stock by 4pm the same day.

Workers marched with placards each morning around Cavendish and Hanover squares supported by cheering crowds. The actress Sybil Thorndike, who had worked at Peter Jones, put on a benefit show for the strikers. Among those who made a donation to their cause was none other than Queen Mary herself. An editorial in *The Times* thundered: 'The shopping public has no sympathy nowadays with obsolete ideas about trade unionism and the right of workpeople to fair treatment.' But John Lewis won his day.

The strike ended and strikers were forced to find employment elsewhere. Largely sympathetic to the strikers, Spedan Lewis looked on from Sloane Square, and learned.

Jones store, which Spedan had been tempted to sell that year to Whiteley's. And then, things began to take a turn for the better, beginning with a reconciliation, after years of mutual antagonism, between father and son. This came about when Spedan produced a grandson, John Hunter Lewis: his grandfather was enchanted. He was much taken, too, with Spedan's lively and highly intelligent wife, Beatrice.

Sarah Beatrice Mary Hunter, five years younger than Spedan, was the daughter of an architect and a graduate of Somerville College, Oxford. She was one of the bright young university graduates Spedan had made a policy of recruiting to Peter Jones. (For a short while, Amy Johnson, who became a famous pioneering aviator, had also been one of them, fresh from Sheffield University.) Beatrice Hunter was inspired by Spedan's ideas. She joined as a boot buyer in 1922, the year John Lewis was persuaded by his wife to have a look at what Spedan was up to in Chelsea. 'The place is a credit to the boy,' he said, 'a very great credit.'

Beatrice had taught English after Oxford before joining the Civil Service and becoming a factory inspector during the war. She found Spedan fascinating, writing to a friend,

> 'Life continues hectic and uncertain … it is nerve wracking because one feels one's whole position hangs on the Chairman's caprice – and he may change his mind any moment, in fact he frequently does … it is a perpetual gamble but anyhow it isn't dull – the whole thing, of course, is more like a Musical Comedy than real life, priceless from morning to night …'

Beatrice Hunter Lewis in 1934. Employed by Spedan Lewis as a boot buyer in 1922, she married him the following year.

The two became tennis partners, and they exchanged badinage as well as serves. 'He told me the other day', she wrote, 'I had a disconcerting way of listening to him with the utmost deference while suggesting all the time in the most delicate way in the world that he was merely blithering.' They were married in October 1923 and set up home in a flat in Harley Street, a son John was born the following year. There were to be two more children – Jill, born in 1927, and Edward, in 1929.

Spedan was increasingly keen to unite the two businesses, but although he was now getting on with his father, this was impossible while the latter was still alive. Oswald, however, agreed to sell his share in the company to Spedan, who took out a loan to settle with him, and so he was now in a very strong position, although playing a long waiting game. In the meantime, Spedan had come up with what would be the John Lewis Partnership's enduring slogan, 'Never Knowingly Undersold'. Although initially conceived as a way of ensuring that buyers got the best price from suppliers, it was soon used to sell the idea to customers that they were not paying more at Peter Jones for the same goods that might be found elsewhere. This was in 1925, when trade was picking up, bonuses were being paid and, with a new flush of confidence, buyers were sent off on increasingly exotic trips. Florence Lorimer, a contemporary at Oxford of Beatrice Hunter, was given £5,500 by Spedan to source carpets in Afghanistan, the Punjab and Kashmir.

Staff at Peter Jones, known as Partners since 1920, received bonuses again, in the form of share promises at the time rather than cash, and were feeling generally confident and well treated, while at John Lewis

Staff from Heelas of Reading set off on a holiday jaunt in 1924. John Lewis bought the shop, once Linen Drapers and House Furnishers to the Prince of Wales, in 1953.

their counterparts remained in fear of the peccadilloes of their venerable chairman. Spedan was still treading on eggshells around his father; an unintentionally funny memo of 25 October 1926 from Spedan to the restaurant manager at John Lewis instructs the latter on what and how to serve him. He must provide very particular large, thin, square water biscuits from Huntley & Palmers along with Parmesan cheese and French dried plums. Service had to be just so.

On 8 June 1928, John Lewis died; Spedan was now sole owner of both businesses. He moved very quickly indeed to create the ideal form of partnership he had been brooding over for many years. He had the business valued at over £1 million. Then, in 1929, with a capital of £312,000, he formed the John Lewis Partnership. This was the First Trust Settlement. The first Partnership constitution ran to no fewer than 268 pages. In brief, profits were to be distributed to all Partners. Spedan would retain personal control of the business but would receive no salary, fees or interest; he would live on £1 million of non-interest-paying loan stock repaid to him over 30 years. In practice, this earned him the equivalent of about £1.5 million a year in today's money, although, as inflation bit from the 1940s onwards, this would have been whittled down to around £500,000 in the 1950s. In practice, he took from the business only what he needed.

Improvements to the business, and to the lot of the Partners, were immediate, despite the fact that the Partnership itself had been constituted in the teeth of the Great Depression that would throw millions out of work and make life a misery for millions more. Spedan introduced a sickness benefits scheme, allowed female shop assistants to dress in green dresses of

PETER JONES

—&—

AMY JOHNSON

Copyright
Ruth Hollick
Photographer
Melb:-

Amy Johnson, the pioneering 'aviatrix' who went on to achieve world fame as a record-breaking long-distance pilot in the 1930s, was one of Spedan Lewis's bright young women recruited in the late 1920s.

Born in Hull, Amy graduated from Sheffield University with a BA in Economics. Her first job was as a solicitor's secretary in London, but in 1928 she was employed as a sales assistant at Peter Jones. In 1929 she gained her pilot's licence and an aircraft – a de Havilland Gipsy Moth – from her doting father. The following May, she flew from Croydon to Darwin, the first woman to make the journey by air, solo, from England to Australia. Many other records came her way.

Sadly, she was shot down and killed by RAF fighters over the Thames Estuary in January 1941 ferrying an aircraft ostensibly from Blackpool to RAF Kidlington, Oxfordshire, while on duty with the Air Transport Auxiliary. Amy is seen, left, in a signed postcard, and, right, in April 1930, preparing the Gipsy Moth for her epic flight to Australia.

their own choice, and offered Partners the run of the estate he had bought in 1926 at Odney on the River Thames at Cookham, Berkshire. The main house there, Lullebrook Manor, became (and remains) a staff hotel.

In 1928, Spedan bought an estate, which included the entire village of Leckford, Hampshire, and moved his family to Leckford Abbas, a modest neo-Elizabethan brick and Bath stone country house designed by the venerable architect and historian Banister Fletcher, and built in 1901. Spedan Lewis' interest in architecture was clearly growing at this time, although at Sloane Square in the following decade it was to lead him in a very different stylistic direction from that of Leckford Abbas.

To boost the new business, Spedan had already recruited some of the cream of the new university graduates. Ordinarily, none of them would have entered 'trade' – a world very often looked down upon by academics and well-bred young graduates – but jobs were scarce once the Depression set in. They were therefore only too keen to sign up with the Partnership, and to participate in Spedan's ideas. They were also lucky in that, far from exploiting the situation in the labour market, he offered generous salaries and good conditions.

Bernard Miller, seen here in 1950, was employed straight from university in the late 1920s.

Bernard Miller was one of these bright young men, employed in 1927 straight from Oxford. He was taken on as a trainee silk salesman. When he proved to be colour-blind, he was moved to Spedan's personal office, becoming the latter's PA. It was Miller who, more than a quarter of a century later, was to succeed Spedan as the Partnership's chairman.

Miller married Jessica ffoulkes, a fellow Partner, whom he met at Odney; he later commented that the company was like a 'marriage mart', with so many young men and women meeting their future spouses there. He also recalled that working for the mercurial Spedan was extremely hard. The chairman, though, was always generous, taking Miller and other young members of staff to dinner at Prunier's, the much-missed French restaurant in St James's, after particularly demanding days.

Spedan chose his new circle of young future principals from any number of backgrounds. Michael Watkins, for example, taken on in 1926, was the son of a railway worker; but he had also been commissioned in the army during World War I at the tender age of 17, serving with the Tank Corps. Having won a scholarship to Cambridge, he left the university with a first-class degree in mathematics. What Spedan admired was brains, not background.

As Charles Reilly, his architect friend, said of Spedan at the time,

> His great invention, the John Lewis Partnership, is to me something like a great university. I have not met, outside the permanent members of a university, men like Michael Watkins, who clearly with a very subtle and acute brain seems to care not only for most of the things my young artist and socialist friends care for, but who takes extreme pains not to tread on other people's feelings. To find such men holding positions of great responsibility in a highly successful business is a great surprise.

Spedan likened his team of all talents to the government's cabinet, expecting its members to argue and debate, and to pull together when decisions had been thrashed out. He said he wanted people who were like catfish, with two very large barbs to tickle other fish up and make them dash around the tank.

They certainly had to dash about as, from 1933, Spedan began buying shops and department stores outside London, beginning with Jessops in Nottingham and Lance & Lance in Weston-super-Mare, followed in 1934 by Tyrrell & Green of Southampton and Knight & Lee of Southsea. The idea was to increase the company's buying power and to help forestall the threat to John Lewis of rapidly growing 'multiples' like Marks & Spencer, which had launched its own 'St Michael' food and clothing label in 1928. John Lewis unveiled its own 'Jonell' – as in 'John' and 'L' for Lewis – range of goods in 1937 (the name was changed to 'Jonelle' later). By now, the rationale for expansion of the business also took account of the fear of what might happen to the London stores if there was another war.

Meanwhile, Odney and the John Lewis social life thrived. Beatrice directed revues, while sports and recreation thrived. At a chess competition in 1938, Spedan was beaten by a 14-year-old boy from a Liverpool secondary school; Spedan was so impressed that he sought out his teacher, Edgar Pennell, and took him on as the Partnership's head of training.

YOUR ROOM
as a BACKGROUND

A circular wooden tub for waste-paper painted in colourings to tone with your room, price 15s. 6d., post free, in U.K. From Helen I. Lamb, 3 Bellevue Parade, Bellevue Road, Wandsworth Common, London, S.W.17.

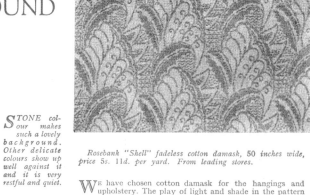

Rosebank "Shell" fadeless cotton damask, 50 inches wide, price 5s. 11d. per yard. From leading stores.

S TONE col-
our makes
such a lovely
b a c k g r o u n d.
Other delicate
colours show up
well against it
and it is very
restful and quiet.

W E have chosen cotton damask for the hangings and upholstery. The play of light and shade in the pattern makes it look very rich against the plain stone walls, and it is very hard-wearing. Piped with blue the chairs are linked up with the colour scheme of the carpet, and the yellow of the cushions gives just the hint of sunny warmth needed in the room.

Above
An illustration of modern furniture from
My Home magazine, 1938.

Opposite
A page from the Peter Jones autumn fashions
catalogue 1926.

In 1935, Spedan decided to 'die' to see how his young management team would cope without his hand on the wheel. They did very well. Spedan offered a number of them, including Michael Watkins, what would be called 'golden handcuffs' today. If Watkins were to sign a contract with John Lewis taking him to retirement at 65, Spedan would pay him a salary, starting at £3,000 (around £160,000 today), with eight weeks' annual holiday and a minimum working week of 30 hours. It was a very generous offer for a young man at a time when the economy had yet to recover. Britain would remain in the red up to, through and long after World War II. Needless to say, Watkins accepted.

In 1937, Spedan decided to branch out into the grocery business, and bought Waitrose, a chain of ten shops in the London suburbs that had established itself as a reliable source of high-quality and unadulterated food. Part of the idea was that Waitrose would supply a new chain of John Lewis hotels, although the war was to put an end to such luxurious thinking.

Waitrose had been founded as Waite, Rose and Taylor in Acton, west London, in 1904. Taylor left the firm early, Rose did the accounts and Waite was the grocer. One of 11 children, Wallace Wyndham Waite was born in 1881, the son of an itinerant railway foreman, one of whose projects had been the construction of a bridge between Bath and Shepton Mallet. For a while, Wallace had attended Shepton Mallet Grammar School, where John Lewis had been a pupil years before.

Like Lewis, Waite was a self-made man. Apprenticed to a grocer called Pegler in Pontypool, South Wales, he dreamed of owning his own shop. And, when he did, it was a special shop: a grocery where no lead would be found in Gloucestershire cheese, no mercury bisulphate in confectionery, no black lead in tea or sand and ashes in loaves of bread. Waitrose thus became a byword for honest groceries, and Waitrose wears its name with justifiable pride today.

In all this expansion out of London, Spedan did not slacken developments at the original Oxford Street store. In 1928, he had snapped up the premises of T J Harries, also on Oxford Street, to be followed eight years later by the purchase of the building formerly occupied by D H Evans. Now the John Lewis store could stretch along two blocks, making it London's biggest shop – twice as large, in fact, as it is today. To supply the big new outlet and its sibling stores, Spedan went on a spree, buying factories that made hats, leather, bedding, furniture and fabric.

The 1930s had been a time of extraordinary growth for the Partnership, with sales doubling between 1932 and 1937, but the business was stretched by the end of the decade. In 1938, Spedan announced that no bonus was to be paid to Partners – something of a shock to the 10,000 staff who had come to rely on top-ups to their annual salaries of between 7 and 10 per cent throughout most of the decade. Many, of course, would have remembered the pay cuts of 1931 as the Partnership steered its way through the depths of the Great Depression, and they had much to be thankful for – not least Spedan's policy of expansion during this difficult time. When war broke out in September 1939, the Partnership was as prepared as it possibly could be for the uncertain and terrifying journey ahead.

GRANTA   **4** Gns.
A slim-fitting model made easy to wear in stock-size by the sash tying at the back.
In Genita (a kind of Jersey-de-Soie). Green, Sapphire or Black.
  Size 40 ins. (hips).

GORDON   **79/6**
In Jersey-de-Soie with a softly gathered bodice and cut on flowing lines.

In Black/White, Black/Red, Navy/White, Brown/Rust.
Sizes 40, 42 ins. (hips).

MALTA   **6½** Gns.
A sleeveless Dress and Jacket adapted from a model by Patou. In several designs of Blue and White printed Crepe-de-Chine.

  Size 40 ins. (hips).

JOHN LEWIS
AND COMPANY LIMITED

1932   MONTHLY SPECIAL NOTICES   **JUNE**

These Monthly Special Notices are sent Free on request.

High fashion at reasonable prices from John Lewis in 1932, although even the green Granta dress cost more than the weekly wage of a London bus driver.

As for Spedan Lewis himself, he had suffered the loss of his son, John, who died from meningitis in 1932 at the age of just eight. The tragedy had been all the worse because Beatrice was pregnant at the time with what would have been their fourth child; she miscarried and was unable to conceive again. The Lewises had two other children, Jill and Edward. They were to recall the increasingly obsessive behaviour of their father. A man fixated with writing memoranda, he even had a secretary on hand at family mealtimes to record his words, so that nothing would be forgotten.

His secretaries well remembered having to stand outside Spedan's door in Hampshire as he shaved while dictating memoranda. For all his kindnesses and high ideals, Spedan Lewis was to remain an autocrat – albeit a benevolent one. Loquacious, dominant, oratorical and, as friends said of him, 'completely unrelaxed', this beautifully mannered perfectionist crackled with energy and liked, at all times, to be the centre of attention, whether at home or at work. And yet, as he expanded, developed and nurtured the business through the 1930s, he was all the while planning to give his ownership and control of it to his principals and Partners – a truly remarkable act for so controlling a man. However, just now was not the moment to let go: Hitler had invaded Poland, and the fight for freedom was on.

SOCIAL UNREST

A deeply depressed economy, deeper social divides, dismal working conditions, women seeking equality with men: these were all potent factors leading to great social upheaval between the two world wars, accompanied by the rise of dark and dangerous political movements.

Previous pages
'Battle of Cable Street', Aldgate, London, 4 October 1936. An anti-Fascist crowd, some of them carrying missiles, run from a barricade they have erected near Aldgate.

Main image
Suffragettes campaigning in central London against the Liberal Party during the general election of January 1910. The Liberals were only just able to form a new government with the support of the Irish Parliamentary Party; a second election was held that December with the Irish coming to the rescue of the Liberals once again.

Vintage colour postcard featuring suffragettes, seeking votes for women, c. 1910.

A million British soldiers and civilians were killed during World War I, a cataclysmic and essentially pointless four-year conflict that witnessed the death, altogether, of 16 million people. Yet the 'Spanish Flu' epidemic that followed proved a more deadly killer even than the Great War itself. Between 20 and 40 million people died from it in 1918 and the following year – 228,000 of them in Great Britain.

Despite a promise from Prime Minister David Lloyd George, leading a Liberal–Conservative coalition government, to make post-war Britain 'a country for heroes to live in', it was clearly no such thing. Nonetheless, the conflict had swept away Edwardian Britain and its grand old ways, exaggerated class divisions and extremes of opulence and destitution – at least in the minds of millions of men and women who had fought long and hard for 'King and Country'. British society had changed considerably over those four years, and now people from all walks of life were going to fight for what Westminster was incapable of giving them. They wanted jobs, pensions, health insurance and proper education, unemployment benefits and, increasingly, equal opportunities and rights.

The collective desire for these things was only intensified by the fact that the Liberal governments of 1906 to 1914 had introduced a stream of reforms intended to help working people and children. Schools had been instructed to provide free meals, although they did not always do so. Children were no longer allowed to beg, sell cigarettes or be sent to prison. The school-leaving age was raised to 14. There were pensions for those over 70. Labour exchanges were set up to help the unemployed find work, while the National Insurance Act of 1911 gave people the right to free medical treatment, sick pay and the dole. But because poor families thought the contributions costly and sick pay poor, they jeered at Lloyd George: 'Taffy is a Welshman, Taffy is a Thief'.

Still, the Liberals tried: school inspections; compensation for injuries caused by work; an eight-hour day for miners; and pay for MPs, so that working men could stand for Parliament. Yet people wanted more.

During World War I women took on many skilled jobs that had been the preserve of men for generations; here, a woman is hard at work making artillery shell cases in a munitions factory in 1915.

Women certainly did. The suffragettes, led by Emmeline Pankhurst, had fought hard for votes for women before the war. They had chained themselves to railings, smashed windows, set fire to postboxes and detonated bombs. They had served time in prison, where they were force-fed during hunger strikes. Most dramatically of all – and partly because the event was caught on camera by Pathé News, and screened at cinemas around the country – Emily Davison, an Oxford graduate and teacher, hurled herself in front of the king's horse, Anmer, at the 1913 Derby. It remains unclear, but she might have been trying to wrap a 'Votes for Women' sash around the horse's neck. She died soon afterwards, a martyr to the suffragette cause; haunted by her face as she fell under his horse, Herbert Jones, the jockey, eventually committed suicide.

The suffragettes' campaign, unpopular at the time, was given an enormous boost not by violent action but by the role that British women played throughout the war. Working in industry, on the railways, as nurses and with the armed forces in a wide variety of roles, as well, of course, as keeping the home fires burning, women proved themselves the equal of men not only in their own eyes but also in those of many politicians – not least Lloyd George. Before 1918 was out, women had won the right to vote and to stand for parliament. Even then, they had to be over 30, and it was to be another ten years before the age limit was lowered to 21 in line with that for men.

Opposite
The first woman elected as an MP to Westminster, in 1918, was the fiery Sinn Fein representative Countess Markievicz, seen here addressing a crowd at Boston, Massachusetts, in May 1922. As a protest against British politics, she had refused to take her seat in the House of Commons.

Right
Margaret Bondfield, a former draper's apprentice, was the first woman to serve in a British cabinet; Ramsay MacDonald appointed her Minister of Labour in 1929.

The general election held in December 1918 witnessed the first woman elected to Westminster. This was Countess Constance Markievicz, the elder daughter of Sir Henry Gore-Booth, an Anglo-Irish explorer and adventurer who had fed tenants for free at his estate at Lissadell House in County Sligo during the famines. Married to a Polish artist, the 50-year-old countess was in Holloway Prison for fighting Irish conscription to the British armed forces at the time of the 1918 election. In the event, like her fellow Sinn Fein MPs she refused to take her seat in Westminster. She had earlier been sentenced to death for her part as a lieutenant in the Irish Citizen Army during the 1916 Easter Rising in Dublin. The sentence had been commuted to life imprisonment, but Lloyd George released her in 1917.

After the death of his father, and as sole owner of the company, in 1929 Spedan set up the John Lewis Partnership. In many ways it was a culmination of the radical ideas that had led to women's liberation and, increasingly, to a belief that everyone from whatever background deserved to do well. The unprecedented five-week strike at John Lewis in 1920 had been a sign that, after the experience of World War I, working people felt justified in pushing their claims. They were restless and looking for the world 'fit for heroes' that the wartime government had promised.

Under Spedan's leadership, wages rose, working hours were cut and great improvements made to staff living conditions. Women graduates were employed alongside men. John Lewis, although paternalistic, was in the forefront of social reform.

Women jurors, meanwhile, made their mark in Britain's courts for the first time in 1920, while in 1922, Ivy Williams became the first female barrister and Marie Stopes opened her first birth-control clinic, at Holloway in north London. Enid Locket, one of the first women to be called to the Bar, was employed as the Partnership's first legal adviser, and worked with Spedan Lewis on the Partnership's constitution. Equal rights in divorce for men and women were granted in 1923, and in 1929, Margaret Bondfield, as Minister of Labour in Ramsay MacDonald's newly elected Labour government, became the first woman cabinet minister. Born in Somerset, she had been apprenticed to a draper in Brighton before making her way into politics as a young trades union official in London.

Women were proving themselves the equal of men whether as academics or adventurers, architects, designers and, of course, actors both on stage and on the silver screen. Vivien Leigh, the singularly beautiful daughter of an Indian army cavalry officer, took the London stage and then Hollywood by storm in the 1930s.

Enid Marx, a distant cousin of Karl Marx and one of Britain's finest textile designers, produced attractive and intensely hard-wearing moquette seating for the London Underground – as did Marion Dorn, a Californian who established her own design agency in London in 1934. From the 1930s, the ceramicist Susie Cooper supplied the Partnership with her work. Meanwhile, Elisabeth Scott, one of a very small number of qualified women architects, was busy at work on the design and construction of the Shakespeare Memorial Theatre at Stratford-upon-Avon.

Then as now it was hard, especially for a woman, to please everyone. The *Manchester Guardian* dismissed Scott's design as 'startling . . . monstrous and brutal', while Sir Edward Elgar, who had been invited to become the theatre's musical director, said that he would refuse to enter the building, referring to Scott as 'that awful female'.

Opposite page
Enid Marx textile designs.

This page
Marion Dorn fabric designs.

Although there was still a very long way to go, the rise and liberation of women between the two world wars had an enormous effect on domestic life, the world of everyday work and the professions, on fashion, design and shopping habits. But, although women had achieved a great deal in those 20 years, for many working people there was precious little to celebrate.

It is easy to be dazzled by newsreels of the era and to think of Britain between the wars as a world of cocktails; jazz; Louise Brooks lookalike short-skirted, bob-haired flappers; Bertie Wooster; mock-Tudor homes; BBC radio presenters dressed in dicky bows; mighty green Bentleys trouncing foreign opposition at Le Mans; Noël Coward plays; and the *Queen Mary* sailing imperiously across the Atlantic. In the early 1920s, the British Empire may indeed have reached its greatest extent – one in four of the world's

people were nominally British subjects – but the streets of the mother country were not exactly paved with gold.

In 1919, as flu continued to kill, thousands of soldiers from distant parts of the empire and its dominions were still stuck, seemingly forgotten, in squalid camps up and down the country. Also that year, Canadian troops – 15,000 of them – rioted at Kinmel Park in North Wales. The police were not exactly happy arresting working men who had only recently slugged it out in some of the worst battles of the war. In fact, the police themselves went on strike that year, as they had done in 1918, and 2,000 officers were dismissed at a time when jobs were scarce. The miners followed in 1921; there was talk of a national strike. The government declared a state of martial law. Troops were sent to the pits to confront strikers. The miners were forced to give in; their pay was cut.

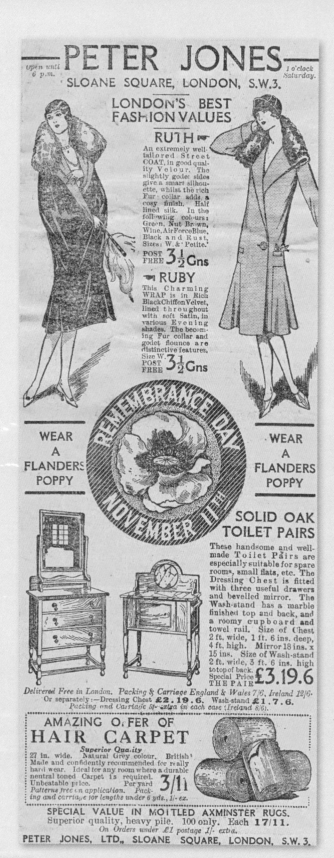

Left
A Peter Jones advert for the latest fashions, in the *Daily Mail*, 1925. The sacrifices of World War I had clearly not been forgotten.

Below
Peter Jones autumn fashion pamphlet, 1926.

FASHIONS FOR AUTUMN

PETER JONES LTD
SLOANE SQUARE, LONDON, S.W.

OCTOBER 1932

Three New Autumn Models from Our Model Coat Department

PRISCILLA. (*left.*) **7½** GNS.
Fancy bouclé woollen cloth, in Navy, Brown, Black, or other colours to special order. The handsome roll collar of Sable-dyed Squirrel is shaped and stiffened to stand up well round the head, and is made unusually long to give a slim line. The lining is artificial Crepe. Sizes W., L.W. and O.S.

PRUDENCE. **6** GNS.
Cumberland Tweed, in two different tones of Brown, with collar of Tasmanian Opossum, or in Grey with Australian Opossum. The collar buttoning across the chest makes this coat very comfortable for cold weather. There are slit pockets at each side and the lining is artificial Silk. Sizes S.W., W. and L.W.

PRISCILLA

PENELOPE. (*right.*) **6¼** GNS.
The material is a fancy woollen, with a faint diagonal weave, in Navy, Brown and Black, or in other colours to special order. The collar is dyed Fox, which is becoming fashionable again. The lining is Artificial Silk. Sizes S.W., W., L.W. and O.S.

JOHN LEWIS & CO., LTD. OXFORD STREET, LONDON, W.1
MAYfair 7711
Page 5

Left
John Lewis catalogue for October 1932, showing the latest lines in fur wraps.

Relationships between workers, employers and government hardened. The Transport & General Workers' Union, Britain's biggest trade union to date, was formed in 1922 with Ernest Bevin as its first general secretary. Born in Somerset, Bevin started work when he was just 11 years old. It would have been impossible to guess, or to believe, at the time, yet this was the man destined to become Minister of Labour in Winston Churchill's wartime coalition government, and, between 1945 and 1951, one of Britain's finest foreign secretaries.

In 1926, however, Bevin and Churchill were at loggerheads. This was the year of the General Strike, when the trade union movement seemed determined as never before to improve what were, all too often, the pitiful wages and conditions of its members. In typically fighting fashion, Churchill, Chancellor of the Exchequer in Stanley Baldwin's Conservative government, said of the impending strike, 'It is a conflict which, if it is fought out to a conclusion, can only end in the overthrow of parliamentary government or in its decisive victory.'

The army and navy were put on alert. Churchill printed a snide propaganda newspaper, the *British Gazette*. University students, up for a lark, volunteered to do manual jobs incompetently. The government declared martial law again, and within nine days the Trades Union Congress surrendered – much to the dismay of millions of its members.

Nonetheless, the Wall Street Crash of 1929 and the Great Depression that followed it took the wind out of the sails of employers, employees and government alike. Westminster, though, remained on its guard for several more years, and perhaps with justification. In 1931, some 1,000

Not a bus in sight, yet this is the morning rush hour at the Royal Exchange in the City of London in 1926. The date is 4 May, during the General Strike, and City workers are making their way to their offices on foot, by bicycle and, of course, by black London cab.

sailors of the British Atlantic Fleet mutinied at Invergordon on the Cromarty Firth in Scotland. Faced with pay cuts, hard-pressed ratings refused to carry out all but essential duties. Many sang 'The Red Flag'. There was panic on the Stock Exchange when the news reached London, and a run on the pound – as if the sailors were about to embark for the Soviet Union or steam down to the Thames to shell the City and Westminster from the London docks. Clearly, many nerves had been frayed by the Wall Street Crash, the General Strike and the rise of communism among British workers in heavy industry and intellectuals in Bloomsbury pubs.

Officers talked sensibly to their crews, and the affair was ended in a typically woolly British compromise. Two hundred sailors were dismissed and the Atlantic Fleet sailed on behind its flagship, the battlecruiser HMS *Hood*. A decade later, the *Hood* was sunk by the German heavy cruiser *Prinz Eugen* and the battleship *Bismarck* in the Denmark Strait, between Iceland and Greenland. Of her 1,418 crew, just three men survived.

The Communist Party of Great Britain was founded in 1920. It never grew to be anywhere near the size of its European counterparts. Membership of the French Communist Party peaked at 800,000; the Italian party topped 1.7 million. The British high was reached in 1943 with no more than 56,000 card-carrying 'Reds'. The party – strongest on Clydeside and in South Wales, East Anglia and east London – did, though, return two MPs to parliament in 1945, although both Phil Piratin (Mile End) and Willie Gallacher (West Fife) lost their seats in the 1950 general election. With Nikita Khrushchev's revelations in 1956 of the cruel excesses of Stalin's regime in the Soviet Union, the controversial Soviet invasion of Hungary that year and radical improvements in living standards at home, support for communism in Britain fell away.

Workers of Crewe in Cheshire
– every last one sporting a hat –
united in favour of the General
Strike, 10 May 1926.

The communists' greatest enemy – a general British antipathy to Marxism aside – was the British Union of Fascists (BUF). This Nazi-style party was founded in 1932. Its membership, which peaked early, numbered about 60,000 – although this had dropped to 20,000 or so at the outbreak of World War II. Who were they? An odd mixture, much like the Nazis themselves, of wealthy landowners, working-class activists and thugs, mild-mannered clerks and seemingly respectable public officials like the poet Philip Larkin's father, treasurer of Coventry city council, who attended Hitler's rallies in Nuremberg. Members attended meetings dressed in black shirts, the name by which the party was known to the media.

The party's founder was Oswald Mosley, an Anglo-Irish aristocrat married to Cynthia, second daughter of Lord Curzon, the former Viceroy of India. When Cynthia died a year after the birth of the BUF, Mosley married his mistress, Diana Guinness (née Mitford). The wedding took place in Joseph Goebbels' home in Berlin. Adolf Hitler was guest of honour.

Nonetheless, the increasing violence of its members at public meetings eventually turned influential supporters away from the BUF. The crunch for the Fascist movement came at the Battle of Cable Street in 1936. As a provocation, the fiercely anti-Semitic Mosley tried to march his Blackshirts – 3,000 strong, and with police protection – through strongly Jewish east London streets. Cockneys, Irish dockers, communists and others fought them back. The police cancelled the march. The Blackshirts had egg on their faces, and on their shirts, too; they had been pelted with eggs, rotten fruit and vegetables. The BUF was banned in 1940.

If the communists and Blackshirts represented the extremes of social unrest in Britain between the two world wars, less violent and media-grabbing protest continued up until 1939 and, even then, there was industrial action during World War II. The arrival in London of the Jarrow March, a 22-day epic trek made by 207 miners from the North East in 1936, revealed something of the true picture of the great social and economic divides that so characterized Britain in the 1920s and 1930s. And officialdom's response was often far from kind.

A popular hunger march held in 1932 against the means-testing of workers seeking the dole, at a time when unemployment stood at 2.75 million, was broken up in Hyde Park by a 70,000-strong police force, and with such heavy-handedness that the National Council for Civil Liberties was founded in response. It is not hard to see why thoughtful people like John Spedan Lewis, and a new generation of newly enfranchised and professional women, were motivated to want to do something to make Britain a better place to live in. It would take another world war and the loss of a further half a million people before Britain became a true social democracy.

An enduring national embarrassment: Britain's would-be *Führer*, Sir Oswald Mosley, gives the Nazi salute to members of his British Union of Fascists, or 'Blackshirts' as they were known, who are seen posing dimly along Royal Mint Street, near the Tower of London.

3

WAR
– & –
REBUILDING

1939–55

At the outbreak of war, John Lewis had 6,000 Partners and an annual turnover of £3 million. The Partnership also had two London department stores, four smaller provincial ones, a central services building in Chelsea, ten branches of Waitrose and a variety of small manufacturing interests bought in the 1930s. The last-named included a hat factory, a leather factory, a chocolate factory and one for making decorated furniture. Lewis had been keen to ensure a supply of goods in times of recession and of slow trading outside the Partnership itself. On Oxford Street, there were two buildings: the T J Harries building, across Holles Street, purchased in 1928 became known as John Lewis East House, while the original shop was called JL West House.

However, in January 1940, at the height of what was known as the 'Phoney War' – nothing much was happening in the war to affect daily life in Britain – the Partnership suddenly doubled its size when it acquired a controlling interest in the ailing SPS Ltd. This was Selfridges Provincial Stores, a company set up by Gordon Selfridge in the 1920s in London suburbs and provincial towns. By 1940, Selfridge was running out of money, so John Lewis was able to snap up his provincial and suburban stores. The 15 outlets brought into the John Lewis fold boosted their buying power and helped ensure that business would continue should anything happen to the London shops in the war. They would also provide employment for Partners forced out of London.

The calm of the Phoney War was shattered on 15 September 1940, when the Luftwaffe began the first of what would turn out to be 1,300 bombing sorties towards London. Buckingham Palace was hit. A German plane crashed into Victoria Station. In his private armoured train across the Channel at Boulogne, Hermann Goering crowed: 'They must be reaching the end of their resources. Today's assault should complete the operation.'

However, Goering had not anticipated the courage of RAF Fighter Command, of whose pilots Winston Churchill had famously declared, 'Never in the field of human conflict was so much owed by so many to so few.' So many German aircraft were destroyed that day that Hitler ordered the cancellation of Operation Sealion – the invasion of Britain. The Battle

Opposite
Prime Minister Winston Churchill inspects the ruins of the House of Commons, destroyed by enemy bombing on 10 May 1941.

Above
John Lewis had been hit by incendiary bombs in September 1940; but the Oxford Street shop, seen here that month, stayed resolutely open.

JOHN LEWIS
AND COMPANY LIMITED.
Oxford Street. W.1.

October 1940.

Dear Madam,

    In the early hours of Wednesday, the 18th September, our business in Oxford Street was hit by several bombs. The damage was very great. Two hundred people were sleeping in our shelter. None of them was hurt at all. But we are very sorry to say that a bomb that fell after the firemen had arrived killed three of them.

    The bombs fell on our West House in the original business that was created by the late Mr. John Lewis. A high wind blew the fire across Holles Street so that much of our East House was destroyed also. The remainder of that building will, we hope, be fit for use almost at once and in that part of the West House that we have just rebuilt against Cavendish Square, the concrete and steel appear to be undamaged, though all woodwork and everything else inflammable has been destroyed completely in this part. If the Government allow us to do the necessary repairs we hope to be doing business. At all events we shall re-open all of our departments just as soon as ever we can, and we hope to make a quite early start, probably within a fortnight, with Piece Goods and some of the more important Dress Accessories, such as Stockings and Lingerie, and a little later, with a good many others, including Furnishing Fabrics, Linen and the principal Fashion Departments.

    In the meantime, as before, we shall be selling at the same prices many of the same goods at Peter Jones in SLOANE SQUARE, S.W.1; John Barnes, FINCHLEY ROAD, N.W.3; Jones Bros., HOLLOWAY ROAD, N.7; Pratts, High Road, STREATHAM; Bon Marché, BRIXTON ROAD, S.W.9; H. Holdron Ltd., Rye Lane, PECKHAM; G.H. Lee & Co. Ltd., Basnett Street, LIVERPOOL; Coles Bros., Church Street, SHEFFIELD; W.J. Buckley & Co. Ltd., Parliament Street, HARROGATE; A.H. Bull Ltd., Broad Street, READING; Robert Sayle & Co. Ltd., 12 St. Andrew Street, CAMBRIDGE; Blinkhorns Ltd., Eastgate Street, GLOUCESTER; Caleys, High Street, WINDSOR; Trewins, Queens Road, WATFORD; Quality Thomsons, Cowgate Street, PETERBOROUGH; Tyrrell & Green, Above Bar, SOUTHAMPTON; Lance & Lance Ltd., Waterloo House, WESTON-SUPER-MARE; and Knight & Lee, Palmerston Road, SOUTHSEA.

    We shall be, of course, very grateful if customers will help us through these difficulties by giving us any business that they can. We shall be able to deal in the regular way with all orders by post addressed to us at Oxford Street. The staff of our Furnishing Departments will wait upon customers in their own homes up to thirty miles from London and at greater distances if the order is substantial. It will be a real help also if account-customers will let us have their cheques as promptly as they can conveniently.

    In accordance with our special partnership-principles on which our business has been conducted for the last ten years, everything possible will be done to prevent hardship for the thousands of people whose livelihood has been thus suddenly destroyed. We shall do our utmost to find work in our other businesses for all who are dependent upon themselves and who cannot get other employment, and everyone will be invited to come back as fast as we can get this great part of our business going again.

    We are, dear Madam,
    Your obedient Servants,
    JOHN LEWIS & CO., LTD.

GENERAL MANAGER.

Opposite

Staff unable to work at Oxford Street after it was bombed were relocated to John Lewis's provincial branches. Clockwise from top left: Windsor must have seemed a very heaven after the blitzed West End, although bombs fell here, too; the streamlined John Barnes department store, Finchley Road, London; W J Buckley, Harrogate; Jones Brothers, Holloway, extended post-war; Jones Brothers, pre-war.

Right

A letter dated October 1940 from John Lewis's General Manager to customers explaining the bombing of the Oxford Street store.

of Britain appeared to be over. As the Luftwaffe's bombers were easy prey to Spitfires and Hurricanes during the day, they started to fly by night. In the early hours of 18 September, an aerial flotilla of 268 bombers flew over London. Bombs were dropped the length of Oxford Street, from Tottenham Court Road to Marble Arch. The John Lewis store was hit by incendiary devices. It took 30 fire engines, and the loss of three firemen, to put out the blaze over the next 36 hours.

    Although Spedan Lewis had felt confident that the war would be over by October 1941, he had nevertheless been preparing for the worst. When the bombs hit the Oxford Street store, some 200 people were sleeping in the makeshift shelter in its basement, so there were no immediate casualties.

    Even before the bombs fell on Oxford Street, sales at Peter Jones had dropped by half as upper-crust shoppers abandoned London for their country estates. They had not abandoned the company, however, as there were many new John Lewis shops (albeit still with their original names) spread around the country. The smallest was Caleys of Windsor. Opened in the town's High Street not far from Windsor Castle in 1823, it had several royal warrants, and Queen Victoria had bought hats there. Further afield, there was Blinkhorns of Gloucester, Buckleys of Harrogate and A H Bull in Reading. Lancashire offered Liverpool's George Henry Lee and Yorkshire Cole Brothers of Sheffield.

Above
Firemen fight the blaze at the Oxford Street store in September 1940; three were killed doing so.

Right
A very relaxed gas-mask drill in an Oxford Street bomb shelter, two years before the bombs fell.

John Lewis selling its wares on Oxford
Street, 1940.

John Lewis stores in the London suburbs included Jones Brothers in Holloway, Holdrons in Peckham, Pratt's in Streatham – once the 'West End' of south London – Brixton's Bon Marché and John Barnes on Finchley Road. These were all shops founded, like John Lewis itself, by drapers. Pratt's, for example, a large and characterful Victorian shop, was built in the 1860s by George Pratt. He had served his apprenticeship in a village drapery shop on the same site when John Lewis was still at school.

Others, like the Bon Marché in Brixton, Britain's first purpose-built department store, had a colourful pedigree. Despite its French name, the shop was the brainchild of Tooting-born James Smith. Smith owned a racehorse, Rosebery, which in 1876 won both the Cesarewitch and Cambridgeshire stakes at Newmarket. With the proceeds, Smith bought a nursery garden on Brixton Hill and, borrowing the name from the original Bon Marché in Paris, set up shop in grand style, selling food as well as furniture, clothes and drapery.

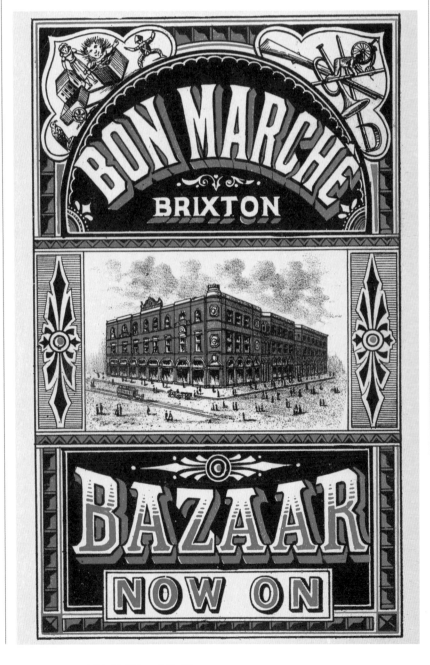

Left
Opened in 1876, the Bon Marché brought Parisian style and flair – as interpreted by its Tooting-born proprietor – to the busy streets of south London. This sales poster is from the late nineteenth century.

Above
The Bon Marché, Brixton, was gutted during a bomb raid in May 1941. It was to reopen, but was sold by John Lewis 30 years after the end of World War II.

Opposite
Because of wartime shortages of materials and labour, the government imposed strict limits on the amount of fabric and labour used in the manufacture of clothing. But 'Utility clothing', as it came to be known, did not have to be dull or unfashionable, and major designers were involved in its creation.

Although Smith was declared bankrupt in 1892, the Bon Marché weathered financial storms, and those of World War II – a bomb hit the shop in May 1941. It was finally sold in 1975, along with several other John Lewis-owned outlets, when the company policy was to stop trading in stores below 18,600 square metres (200,000 square feet).

Remarkably, more shops were taken into the John Lewis fold between 1942 and 1945, in London, Edinburgh, Hull and Newcastle upon Tyne. Local John Lewis staff councils were set up, along with committees for communications to bring the newly acquired premises into line with the London stores. The job of integrating the provincial and suburban shops into the Partnership fell to Sebastian Earl, who had joined the John Lewis Partnership as editor of *The Gazette* in 1932.

Before moving into retailing, Earl had won a silver medal in the Men's Eights at the 1920 Summer Olympics in Antwerp – the first Olympic Games to be staged after World War I – and he certainly needed to keep fit in his new post. Getting around Britain during the blackouts, when mainline trains were crowded with troops and restricted to 100 kilometres (60 miles) per hour, was a feat of endurance. Appointed Director of Expansion in 1946, Earl left the company the following year.

Other senior members of staff were kept frantically busy, not least Michael Watkins, Director of Trading. As well as serving on various official wartime committees, Watkins was appointed Director General of Civilian Clothing. He devised and ran the Utility scheme (which was later extended to furniture) while also working for John Lewis. The Utility scheme was a way of producing clothing within the draconian wartime restrictions on materials (needed elsewhere, for military uniforms and kit). It was a great success, was stocked by John Lewis, and involved the talents of leading fashion designers – among them Norman Hartnell, Hardy Amies, Digby Morton, Bianca Mosca of Jacqmar and Victor Stiebel (who supplied designs while on active war service from 1940 to 1945). Because so many skilled clothing workers had been called up to fight, national standards had to be set for manufacturing quality. Equally, prices had to be kept to a minimum and garments had to be long-lasting. All this fell on Watkins' shoulders. He was rewarded with a knighthood in the New Year's Honours List of 1947. The Utility scheme continued during the years of post-war austerity, ending in 1952. Watkins died in 1950.

Clothing restrictions, and in particular shortages of stockings, combined with a change in the perception of women as they took up wartime roles with assurance and aplomb meant that female staff were allowed to wear slacks in John Lewis offices at much the same time as Watkins was developing the Utility clothing scheme. Nonetheless, this privilege was restricted: women were still not allowed on the shop floor in anything other than a skirt or dress. This even applied to those working on the temporary shop floor in Oxford Street, installed after the bomb damage had been cleared.

Despite the pressures of war, prospects for Partners continued to look up. In 1941, Spedan Lewis promised a generous pension scheme. Those who were called up or volunteered to serve in the armed forces had their pay made up to their normal earnings in 'Civvy Street'. Many Partners felt that this privilege should not be extended to conscientious objectors

JOHN LEWIS
EMPLOYEES
AT
BLETCHLEY
PARK

Conel Hugh O'Donel Alexander (1909–74) was a brilliant Irish-born chess player and mathematician seconded in 1940 to the British government's top-secret code-breaking department at Bletchley Park, a late-Victorian country house near Milton Keynes. Working under Alan Turing – the father of theoretical computer science and artificial intelligence – he helped to break the complex Nazi military Enigma Codes.

Having given up teaching maths at Winchester College in 1938, Alexander had been appointed Head of Research at the John Lewis Partnership, one of the very brightest of the young men and women employed by Spedan Lewis in the 1920s and 1930s. Alexander may well have been instrumental in encouraging Lewis to offer space on the top floor of the Oxford Street store to the National Chess Centre. As a number of Spedan's graduate employees were serious chess players, it seems likely – although secrecy was and remains the name of the game – that Alexander took several other Partners to work with him at Bletchley Park.

Nothing John Lewis might offer, however, could bring this highly intelligent man back into the Partnership's fold in 1945. Alexander became head of 'Section H', the cryptanalysis, or code-breaking, arm of GCHQ until his retirement in 1971.

John Lewis's Director of Trading, Michael Watkins, was in charge of Utility clothing and furniture for the government: the results were plainly excellent.

From 'Satin Silk Food' to the 'Masque of Youth': restricted wartime luxuries from John Lewis's own-brand range of 'Jeanne Louise' beauty preparations.

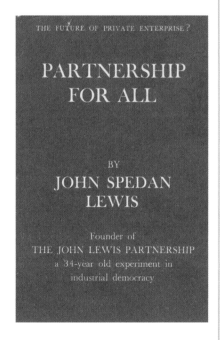

THE FUTURE OF PRIVATE ENTERPRISE?

PARTNERSHIP
FOR ALL

BY
JOHN SPEDAN
LEWIS

Founder of
THE JOHN LEWIS PARTNERSHIP
a 34-year old experiment in
industrial democracy

Title page from *Partnership for All*, 1948, by Spedan Lewis.

working in various forms of war service. The company board made it plain that it was against 'subsidizing' conscientious objectors, but Lewis believed strongly that the values of the Partnership were under threat. He wrote: 'I believe that if the Partnership gives subsidy to conscientious objectors its action will be in keeping with those countless other unreasonable, quixotic actions that have helped make the history of the British people a book in which today we can have some pride.' There was a vote on the matter, with Spedan Lewis casting his chairman's vote in favour of those who believed it was wrong to take another's life in any circumstances.

At the time, he was thinking of Paul Roake, a Partnership salesman and a Quaker (member of the Religious Society of Friends). Roake volunteered to serve with a Friends' Ambulance Unit in Finland. He was in the thick of the action during the Winter War, when the Finns held off the military might of Stalin's Soviet Union.

With the Winter War over, Roake and his fellow Quakers drove their 20 ambulances into Norway to serve there, but were driven back by invading German forces. They were forced to escape back to England on crowded and dangerous ships, but got away in the nick of time. Roake was commissioned, and went on to serve in an ambulance unit in the Middle East.

In a lesson to all staff, Spedan wrote:

Some conscientious objectors are loathsome humbugs. Some are silly fools. Some are the very cream of mankind, people who combine utter unselfishness, extreme kindliness and magnificent courage.

German bombing, meanwhile, destroyed the shops at Southampton and Weston-super-Mare, acquired in the 1930s. When peace came, there was a lot to do in order to get John Lewis back up and running. There were stores in need of rebuilding. There were Partners returning from active service, and a need to recruit new staff. There was a shortage of raw materials. Fuel was rationed. Petrol was rationed. The railways were run-down. The country was bankrupt. But many British people did share a dream of a better country than the one they had known in the impoverished 1930s. As a result, in July 1945 they voted Churchill out and elected a Labour government under Clement Attlee, who had served as deputy prime minister during the war, with a landslide majority.

Churchill and his fellow Tories were shocked. Was this the way the country chose to repay their idol's largely brilliant war leadership? That, though, was not the point. Many voters associated the Tories with the Depression, unemployment, class division and a lack of fairness. Labour promised a Welfare State, government spending to renew Britain's battered infrastructure, a National Health Service and a sense that the old inequalities would be a thing of the past. Spedan Lewis was in tune with the new thinking despite never expressing his personal political view. It was time for him to take the John Lewis Partnership one step further: in 1950 he would transfer the entire ownership and control of the company to the Partners, completing the process he had begun in 1929. And, in doing so, he would write himself out of the Partnership.

THE START OF VE-DAY

HULTON'S NATIONAL WEEKLY
In this issue:
VICTORY SPECIAL 4ᴰ
MAY 19, 1945   Vol. 27, No. 7

Left
Mother and children celebrating
VE (Victory in Europe) Day on the
cover of *Picture Post*.

Opposite
A crowd of soldiers, airmen, sailors and
'civvies', some in funny hats, make their way
into Trafalgar Square for VE Day celebrations,
8 May 1945.

First, however, Lewis and his senior management did their utmost to get the company back into shape. The Partnership needed to make more of the goods that it sold in its stores, and so a factory making quilts and bedding, trading under the name Taylor & Penton, and set up in Chelsea in 1935 was moved in 1945 to Addlestone in Surrey. The following year, Spedan transferred ownership of Leckford to the Partnership. In 1947, well-designed branch newsletters were published under the title *Chronicles*. And in 1948, Spedan published *Partnership for All*, a book setting out what had been achieved to date and what the future held in store.

This was Spedan's manifesto. It is a long book, with 475 pages divided into 29 chapters. Every paragraph of each chapter is numbered; there are 723 in all. It is rather too legalistic for easy reading, but its message was clear. The final paragraph reads:

> . . . so far as general conditions in this country may allow, we should begin now to see how far Producer Co-operatives of this general type may be the answer to one of the great problems of our modern civilisation, how to make our working-lives as fruitful for ourselves and in all other ways as happy as they ought to be and so make ourselves work as well as for our own sakes we should.

THE
POTTERY WORKSHOP
–AT–

ODNEY

Odney is an extraordinary place, largely unknown to the public and yet at the very heart of the life and times of the John Lewis Partnership both yesterday and today. It is an estate of historic refurbished and new buildings beside the River Thames at Cookham, Berkshire. Hidden behind walled gardens, here is a graceful hotel for all Partners, as well as a clubhouse, restaurants, a boating lake, the John Lewis Partnership Archive and much more.

Outside the Partnership, the name Odney is best known for the Odney pottery workshop. From 1942 to 1956, the estate was home to this wartime initiative of Spedan Lewis, which aimed at providing jobs for disabled workers or ex-servicemen as well as high-quality, low-cost earthenware products for John Lewis shops. Set up by John Bew, a civil servant-turned-ceramicist, the pottery did produce work of lasting quality, but was never able to pay its way, and was closed in 1956, although the building itself still exists. Bew himself had vanished two years earlier, and was found drowned. Today the pottery is much sought after, while the estate offers a tranquil retreat for Partners; it is a happy place, an outward sign of the Partnership's well-meaning and philanthropic spirit.

On 26 April 1950, a Second Trust Settlement was signed, transferring power and ownership from Spedan Lewis to the Partnership. Over the next five years – before the 'Founder' (of the Partnership) was due to retire – three fabric shops were opened, and closed, in South Africa; Waitrose Southend went self-service; and more factories were bought or built to produce fabrics in Darwen, Lancashire, and Huddersfield in Yorkshire. Bonuses – cancelled for the duration of the war – returned, but several smaller shops bought from Gordon Selfridge were closed.

On a lighter note, a sailing club was set up under the direction of Geoffrey Snagge, pre-war editor of *The Gazette*. An Indian jute merchant (and trooper in the Calcutta Light Horse regiment) before joining John Lewis in 1933, Snagge had served with distinction with the Royal Navy in World War II. Starting with the purchase of the *Ann Speed*, the club would go on to own five yachts based on the River Hamble near Southampton. Any Partner was able to try their hand on deck. The club eventually became a Royal Yachting Association training school, producing a fair number of fully qualified skippers. It continues today, allowing Partners easy access to what is usually an elite sport.

In 1951 Attlee's Labour government was voted out and in July 1954 rationing came to an end. The economy began to pick up and consumer goods became freely available. In 1957 in came Harold Macmillan's government, along with teenagers; rock 'n' roll; two-tone cars with fins; and televisions, dishwashers and refrigerators – all on hire purchase. In, too, came independence for former British colonies, and immigrants came to take up jobs in an economy boasting low inflation and a shortage of labour.

Below
Contemporary artist's perspective of the Festival of Britain on London's South Bank, dominated – in a blaze of colour – by the Dome of Discovery and the Royal Festival Hall. In comparison, old city streets are made to look monochrome and grim.

Opposite
Abram Games designed the logo for the 1951 Festival of Britain, emblazoned here on the cover of the official guidebook.

SOUTH BANK EXHIBITION

LONDON

FESTIVAL OF BRITAIN

GUIDE PRICE 2/6

Men's wear

for

Autumn

Knight & Lee

70 Elm Grove, Southsea

Portsmouth 74163

Leaflet for autumn menswear
from Knight & Lee, Southsea, 1953.

Britain had been riding on a new high since the coronation of young Queen Elizabeth II in 1953. Edmund Hillary and Tenzing Norgay 'conquered' Everest, England regained the Ashes from Australia and British jets were winning world records; in 1954 Roger Bannister ran a mile in under four minutes. There was a feeling – expressed in the illustrated pages of *The Eagle* comic, with its centrefold cutaway drawings of heroic British machinery and engineering – that Britain had emerged from the war and years of austerity with a terrific future ahead of it, a future as a leading manufacturing nation, and beacon of liberal democracy and all-round decency.

In 1955 Spedan Lewis retired. It was a sad and even tragic parting for him. His surviving son, Edward, had turned him down in favour of practising law when asked to take on the chairmanship. Far worse, in 1953, Beatrice had died from cancer. Spedan scattered her ashes at sea. He wrote:

> *I was stunned by the loss, so utterly unexpected and in so terrible a way,*
> *of the wife to whom in our last years together I said more than once that*
> *I could be well content to spend any years that might remain to me on*
> *a desert island with no company but hers.*

The Partnership had been Spedan's life's work, and he found it very hard to let go. But the Partnership was about to enter new years of prosperity and growth – not just because the economy was booming, but also because Spedan had ensured that it was in capable hands.

A farewell presentation for Spedan Lewis (seated, left) held at Oxford Street on the occasion of his retirement in 1955. His successor, Bernard Miller, is standing behind the flowers on the right.

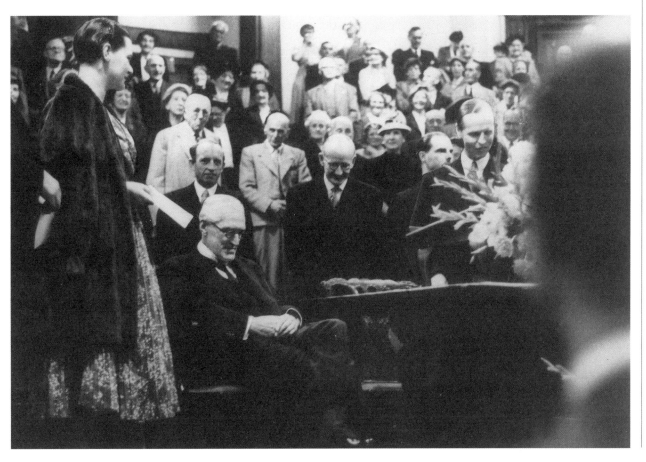

ARCHITECTURE

Spedan Lewis's expenditure on new buildings was both expansive and inspired. The 1930s Peter Jones at Sloane Square remains a model of modern department store design, while in recent decades, John Lewis has experimented with architectural styles.

W hen Spedan Lewis turned his attention to architecture, he appears to have been thinking of building a cathedral of commerce, or shrine to shopping. In his book *Partnership for All*, published in 1948, he wrote:

> In 1933 the Partnership set to work upon its first important building. For this we devised a new technique. It had the hearty benediction of the late Sir Charles Reilly, famous for his development of the School of Architecture in the University of Liverpool. He said that our idea seemed to be a reversion to the methods of the cathedral builders of the Middle Ages.

Sir Charles meant that the functional new Modernist architecture, with its clean lines and machine-like massing, expressed itself as honestly and as openly as medieval Gothic cathedrals once had. Modernism had arrived in Britain from continental Europe in one direction, and from the United States in the other – generally, in concrete form from the former and steel-framed, skyscraper guise from the latter. In 1923, the great French-Swiss Modernist Le Corbusier – chief propagandist for the smooth-walled, concrete tendency – had published a book, *Towards a New Architecture*. In this 'Brave New World' manifesto, 'Corb' had compared the new machine-like twentieth-century buildings with Greek temples, ocean liners, racing cars, aircraft and – yes – medieval cathedrals.

Although such comparisons, brought to his attention by Professor Reilly, must have enchanted Spedan Lewis, he was drawn as much to the down-to-earth American approach to modern design and construction as he was to grand historical comparisons and seductive architectural theory. He wrote:

> Mr Selfridge had once casually remarked to me that the efficiency of building in Great Britain suffers badly because our architects do not work to the extent, that is customary in America, with steel engineers. There the designing of the steel is an integral part of the designing of the building. Suppliers of steel can therefore be asked to tender in a truly competitive way upon a precise design . . .

However, Spedan Lewis would have been fooling himself if he was looking for a low-cost, efficient, modern, new Peter Jones store fronting Sloane Square and King's Road, Chelsea. What he commissioned from William Crabtree, one of Professor Reilly's bright young stars from Liverpool University, was a supremely elegant and costly building that was as much handcrafted as machine-made. Spedan even set up his own John Lewis construction company to realize Crabtree's understated masterpiece.

It had been a fine decision. Although far removed from Selfridge's cut-throat engineering production, the 1937 Peter Jones store was a shining example of how an otherwise big and uncompromising Modernist building

Below
Professor Charles Reilly (1874–1948), a friend of Spedan Lewis, recommended one of his bright young pupils, William Crabtree, from Liverpool University to design the new Peter Jones store.

Bottom
Crabtree, seen here in the 1960s in front of the critically acclaimed 1930s Chelsea store.

Opposite
King George V and Queen Mary drive past the new Peter Jones store under construction in 1935.

JUBILEE DRIV
H.M. KING GEORG
PASSING
REBUILDING O
PETER JONES
SLOANE SQ.

Above
The structural framework of the new Peter Jones store nears completion, 1935. This was a radical design for the era, and must have seemed shocking to passers-by.

Left
The gleaming new, streamlined Peter Jones is seen here in 1937 in all its shipshape architectural and retail glory.

can fit happily into a traditional city street. The close-coupled rhythm of its window frames and structural bays matches the pace of pedestrians as the building 'steps' along the street, in much the same way as the proportions and facades of Georgian buildings do. Internally, it gave Spedan Lewis exactly what he wanted: abundant daylight; a free-flowing, flexible interior; and maximum display-window space at pavement level. Today, the store is listed Grade II* and in 2004 it was intelligently restored and remodelled internally by the architects John McAslan + Partners.

By now, John Lewis had caught the architecture 'bug'. The executive architects of Peter Jones – in charge of working drawings and day-to-day design and construction – were Slater and Moberly. Teamed up with Reginald Uren, a young architect from New Zealand, the practice went on to win the commission to design a new John Lewis headquarters in Oxford Street in 1938.

This new 'parent' store, faced in stone, was only partially completed before a German bombing raid on 18 September 1940. All but the Cavendish Square frontage was destroyed. After the war, Slater, Moberly and Uren designed a new building fronting Oxford Street. This has a very different feel and character to the pre-war edifice facing Cavendish Square. The latter had something of an ocean liner in its design, with its stepped-back upper decks and round windows like portholes.

The new Oxford Street building – designed in 1954, built between 1958 and 1965 and the first part officially opened in 1960 – is a powerful composition – like the Classical city blocks of Renaissance Italy. Its massive six-storey street frontage – the top floor is recessed – is formed of 11 bays, three on one side and seven on the other of a great stairwell that makes the eleventh. The bays are divided by tall vertical window frames; as at Peter Jones, these break up what would otherwise be too horizontal a facade and help 'pace' what is a very big and bold, concrete-framed building along Oxford Street.

In recent years, the store has been treated to a major £61.5 million makeover. Under the design direction of architects Wilson Mason and Partners, a central atrium has been opened up. It is served by banks of silent escalators – lowered through the roof with 10mm (less than half an inch) to spare on either side – offering customers far-reaching views into departments on different floors as they glide up and down. Since 2007, the Oxford Street store has boasted a new food hall, a fifth-floor restaurant with windows overlooking stretches of the West End, and a third-floor brasserie. Today, the building's interior gleams as never before, as does *Winged Figure*, the recently cleaned and restored sculpture on the Holles Street side of the store.

The chairman, Bernard Miller, commissioned this much-loved sculpture as part of the John Lewis centenary celebrations in 1964. It had begun with a competition, yet Miller felt none of the entries said anything particular, or special, about the Partnership. He asked Barbara Hepworth, the celebrated Yorkshire-born artist, to lunch, suggesting that the sculpture should 'have some content that expresses the ideas of common ownership and common interests in a partnership of thousands of workers'.

After she had thought about the idea, Hepworth proposed a much bigger version of her *Winged Figure 1* of 1957. The new version for Oxford Street, installed in 1963 at a cost of £7,000, was to be 5.8 metres (19 feet 3 inches) high and set on a pedestal 4 metres (13 feet) above the pavement. Crafted in Hepworth's studio in St Ives, Cornwall, *Winged Figure 2* was an ultra-modern design, realized in sheet aluminium and stainless-steel rods. Hepworth said that the wings represented Capital and Labour, connected by the steel rods: at John Lewis, the two were not set apart, but worked hand-in-hand, both essential, both equal partners in the enterprise. More poetically, Hepworth said,

> I think one of our universal dreams is to move in air and water without the resistance of our human legs. I wanted to evoke this sense of freedom. If the *Winged Figure* in Oxford Street gives people a sense of being airborne in rain and sunlight and nightlight I will be very happy.

Above
William Crabtree was greatly influenced by the superb new Schocken stores in Germany designed by Erich Mendelsohn. The Stuttgart Shocken opened in 1928; despite international protest, it was demolished in 1960.

Opposite
Many of the most modern department stores of the 1930s were to be found in Berlin. This is the F V Grünfeld store on Kurfürstendamm during the 1928 *Berlin im Licht* (Berlin in Light) festival; it was designed by the architect and graphic artist Otto Firle.

PROTOS

PROTOS ELEKTRISCHE DIENT HAUSGERÄTE

PROTOS BOHNER DER BÜGELEISEN

PROTOS STAUBSAUC R HAUSFRAU TURBOWASCHER PR

F.V.GRÜNFELD

Above
Unexecuted design for the new 1930s John Lewis store on Oxford Street by William Crabtree. This is the view from Cavendish Square.

Left
Crabtree's design as it would have looked from Oxford Street. The design was never built, as it was too radical for the landlord, the Howard de Walden estate.

It is said that the sculpture is looked at by 200 million people a year – although the truth is that many Oxford Street shoppers hurry along the crowded pavements, rarely stopping to look up. Even so, perhaps more people are doing so again now that the 50-year-old artwork has been cleaned and restored to its original lustre.

Despite his protégé's big break on the Peter Jones store, the venerable Sir Charles Reilly – Spedan's original advisor, all those years ago – had not lost out entirely. Spedan had commissioned from him an ambitious design for a new complex of staff hostels, hotels and club buildings at Odney, Berkshire. The scheme was never built, yet the drawings, submitted in 1927, survive in the John Lewis Partnership's Archive at Odney. This is housed in a delightfully modest yet highly intelligent building stitching together old and new architecture into a happy quilt of a design, far removed from Reilly's bombastic scheme.

For several decades after the completion of the new Oxford Street store at a cost of £7 million (£130 million at the time of writing), John Lewis took something of a back seat in terms of architectural design. There were, though, some important projects: the listed warehouse at Stevenage, designed by Felix Candela, was state-of-the-art and is the only example of his work in the country; the department store at Kingston upon Thames, which combines a John Lewis and a Waitrose, won several architectural awards, the major road running through the building's footprint proving a distinct architectural challenge. Increasingly, John Lewis's future stores were housed in new shopping centres and malls, where the architectural design was a given. What mattered most here was the flow of internal space and the maximum amount of display for goods. But, when Selfridges opened its sensational, eye-catching new outlet in Birmingham's Bull Ring in 2003, it was clearly time for rival department stores to think again.

The new escalators gliding up and down the light and airy central atrium of the Oxford Street store, providing views into refurbished departments on every floor.

Below
Early nineteenth-century fabric, commissioned by the Covent Garden draper Richard Ovey and found in the John Lewis textile archive in Carlisle, the inspiration for the look of the new John Lewis Leicester, opened in 2008.

Bottom and opposite
The new Leicester store, designed by Foreign Office Architects, with its striking decorative metal-and-glass facade.

After all, consumer tastes appeared to have changed, and – pre-credit crunch – there was a marked shift away from discretion to 'bling' in the goods on offer and the design of many new shops. Should stores be polite architectural containers for heavily marketed 'brands', or should they adopt the culture and aesthetic of the goods they stock?

In 2008, John Lewis unveiled a new Leicester store alongside busy Vaughan Way. With its hundreds of mirror-finished swirls and curls, the new building referenced the products of Leicester's famous hosiery and fabric industries, which are also a part of the John Lewis story and sold in John Lewis stores up and down the country. So perhaps it should come as little surprise that this store appears to have been cut and pasted from a giant roll of fabric, or even hosiery.

In fact, its striking facade *was* derived from a fabric design, one commissioned in 1803 by Richard Ovey, a London linen-draper. The architects found it in the John Lewis textile archive. As Farshid Moussavi and Alejandro Zaera-Polo – founding partners of Foreign Office Architects (FOA) – explained at the time of the building's completion, this fabric effect was to give the building's bulk a 'layered transparency'. It might also be read, they said, as a net curtain or a play on traditional Indian decoration, a nod to the city's sizeable Asian population.

More prosaically, the screen acts as a sunshade, necessary since the walls of the four-floor store are almost all glazed. While FOA's decorative treatment is undeniably beguiling, this is really entertaining dress-up design, the

The view along the King's Road
from the terrace at Peter Jones.
The shop stayed open throughout
the remodelling work, which was
completed in the summer of 2004.

cladding of a big developer's building in architectural fancy dress. This approach to design has become increasingly common as major stores set up shop in giant shopping malls where the buildings are, for the most part, a *fait accompli* and all an individual company's architects and designers can do is to dress them up.

The recent renovation and remodelling of Peter Jones in London, however, has shown that John Lewis's commitment to architecture and urban design had deep roots. Here the opportunity was taken, at significant cost, not only to renew the 1930s structure, but also to connect it seamlessly with the four other Peter Jones buildings clustered around it and dating from between 1895 and 1965. These include an exquisite Arts and Crafts house dating from 1899, designed by Arthur Heygate Mackmurdo – a contemporary of Charles Rennie Mackintosh.

This remodelling was in stark contrast to the interior of the Crabtree store, which, although as popular as ever with shoppers, had grown tired 60 years on from its opening. There were too many changes in floor levels and fluctuations in temperature, access for goods was poor and a host of other minor grumbles had surfaced over the years. Although John Lewis had wanted to bring the Grade II*-listed building complex up to date for some while, it was concerned that if the shop closed for too long it would lose staff and customers to rivals. So, it decided on an ambitious seven-year programme to renovate the building while customers carried on shopping.

Those parts of the Victorian structures that could be gutted without aesthetic loss have been cleared up, with approval from the heritage lobby, so that floors across the complex now line up with one another for the first time. Selling space has been increased by over 20 per cent. The shop's floors are punctuated by a bright new six-storey atrium criss-crossed with smoothly operating escalators and crowned by a 270-seat self-service cafe with sweeping views across west London. An expensive air-cooling system, easy access for goods and a general rationalization all contribute to what is now, once again, one of Britain's smartest shops.

John McAslan, architect of the scheme, greatly admires the way in which Crabtree's 1930s design 'steps' at a very human pace around Sloane Square and down King's Road, rather than stretching uncomfortably along the street as so many computer-designed commercial buildings would do today.

This subtlety of composition is why, no matter how 'modern' his design might have been when first built, Crabtree's building has always been a good companion to its tall, thin nineteenth-century neighbours. And just as well, for this is where many of the shop's core customers lived, and continue to live; it was good to have enticed them with exciting new design, but not to the point of offence, as might have happened in less skilled hands.

In their design of Peter Jones, Crabtree and Spedan Lewis broke away confidently from the grandiloquent architecture of early London department stores – Harrods, Selfridges and Whiteley's among them. The success of this great institution, and to a lesser extent the John Lewis store on Oxford Street, is a reflection of its ability to be exciting and modern, yet comfortable and reassuring at one and the same time – a difficult trick to pull off, but done so well for John Lewis by Crabtree and co.

4

THE
CONSUMER
BOOM

1955–72

*Go around the country, go to the industrial towns, go to the farms and you
will see a state of prosperity such as we have never had in my lifetime, nor
indeed in the history of this country . . . indeed let us be frank about it –
most of our people have never had it so good.*

This was Harold Macmillan, the prime minister, speaking at a Conservative
party rally held in Bedford in July 1957. Spedan Lewis had retired
two years earlier, and Bernard Miller was now chairman of the John
Lewis Partnership.

From 1955, there had indeed been a change in Britain's fortunes.
Rationing had finally come to an end the previous summer. Hire purchase
allowed working people to buy furniture, cameras, bicycles, domestic
appliances and cars for the first time – and in huge numbers. Commercial
television, launched in 1955, brought adverts into the nation's living rooms
as never before. The rise of the new 'Consumer Society' was beginning.
With money to spend, increasingly knowledgeable customers could weigh
up the merits of Sony's brand-new TR-63 transistor radio – so small that
it could slip into the pocket of a shirt – and the 'must-have' Dansette. This
bright red, folding-topped record player became a feature of thousands of
teenagers' bedrooms.

People were much better off in the Sixties than they had been
before, and there was so much more for them to choose from, whether
in food, fashion, furniture, film, holidays, cars, music or 'lifestyles'. More
shoppers than ever began to buy with credit cards – Barclaycard appeared
in 1966, followed by the Access card in 1972. As important was the sense of
freedom and opportunity offered to people up and down the country. The
1960s was the age when Cockney snappers like David Bailey and Terence
Donovan turned celebrated *Vogue* fashion photographers. The models, such
as Twiggy, who now graced the pages of fashion magazines came from
similar backgrounds themselves as, of course, did many pop stars and
film stars. Meanwhile, a host of new university graduates, many of them
from working- and lower-middle-class families, entered the job market at
the very moment when there were so many interesting new ways to earn

Jean Shrimpton, aged 17, a demure English rose
in a halterneck, rose-patterned chiffon cocktail
dress photographed in 1960 by Norman
Parkinson. Within two years, photographed for
Vogue by David Bailey, she would be fashion's
face of the Swinging Sixties.

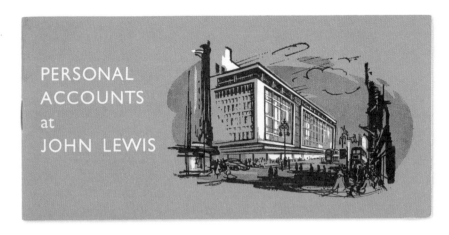

PERSONAL
ACCOUNTS
at
JOHN LEWIS

Access helps you buy
that special Christmas present.
At Christmas.

Christmas comes but once a year so
naturally you want to make the most of it.

But Christmas can be a trying time
financially. Because your budget has to
accommodate everything from pudding to
presents.

Access helps you spread the load.

With it you can buy the things you
want and pay for them over a period of time.

That way you can buy your son the
bike you'd like him to have, rather than give
him a smaller present along with a promise.

And that way, no-one needs to be
disappointed.

You can use an Access card wherever
you see the Access symbol.

It's on more than sixty-thousand shops
and stores throughout Britain.

Access takes the waiting out of wanting.

Access

4987 910 25436 18
MR JOHN G BEVAN
Expires end 12 / 73

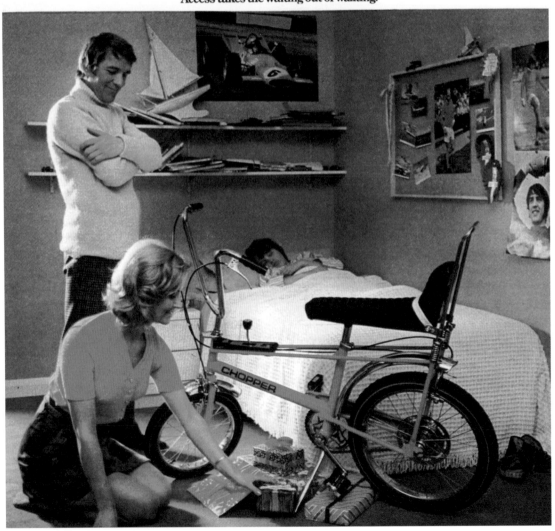

John Lewis account mailers from the 1950s
included with customer account bills:
a celebration of the consumer boom that
followed long years of austerity and rationing.

a living: advertising, marketing, public relations, television, fashion and glossy as well as 'alternative' magazines.

Bernard Miller and the John Lewis Partnership were to benefit hugely from the uplift in the economy from 1955 to 1972, when the Oil Crisis dawned. The company transformed itself from a remarkable and brave experiment in ownership and control into a thriving business. Miller turned Spedan Lewis' dream into a highly successful retail business and made the idea of workers' participation a reality. When he took over, there were 12,000 Partners and sales of £28 million; when he retired, aged 68, in 1972, sales had risen to £140 million, and there were 20,000 Partners. The Waitrose food chain grew over the same period from 3 to 43 supermarkets. Annual staff bonuses averaged 13.5 per cent during the Miller years, topping 18 per cent in 1972. There had been new acquisitions along the way, including a textile-printing works, and technological innovations, among them computerized stock control.

Miller's first year as chairman coincided with the rebuilding of the Oxford Street store and the opening of the first custom-designed new-generation Waitrose, at Streatham, south London. The new chairman was concerned throughout his tenure to ensure that high standards prevailed in design, business and staff conditions. He wanted the best for the company he was to serve for nearly half a century.

Left
Which shiny new kettle should these ladies choose? Cover of first edition of *Which?*, the Consumers' Association magazine, autumn 1957.

Above
Made in London, the red and white portable Dansette record player was a 1960s favourite.

Opposite
Archetypal Teddy Boy in crepe jacket, surrounded by more soberly dressed pals.

Which?

?

Autumn, 1957
Published by
Consumers' Association Ltd
Reprinted September 1960

Barbara Hepworth

The striking sculpture *Winged Figure*, which adorns the north-east corner of John Lewis Oxford Street, was commissioned for the firm's centenary in 1964. It is the work of Barbara Hepworth, one of Britain's finest modern sculptors. From the late 1920s her work, both large- and small-scale abstract pieces, was influenced by the sculpture of European masters such as Picasso and Brancusi. She is known through her many public commissions, particularly in the UK.

Hepworth was famous by the time, in spring 1961, she agreed to Bernard Miller's commission to create one of her very largest pieces – 5.8 metres (19 feet 3 inches) high. Quite what it represents is, with hindsight, rather hard to say. Hepworth said that the two aluminium wings, joined together by steel rods, symbolized the union of Capital and Labour, although she also said: 'I think one of our universal dreams is to move in air and water without the resistance of our human legs. I wanted to evoke this sense of freedom.' Significantly, her eldest son, Paul, was killed in an aircraft crash in 1953 while serving with the RAF. That winged machine would have been made of aluminium and steel. Hepworth died in a fire in her Cornish studio in 1975. Her talent is celebrated not only in *Winged Figure* – since refurbished – but also in The Hepworth Wakefield, opened in 2011, and at the Barbara Hepworth Museum in St Ives. The Tate also has a substantial collection of her work.

Royal Blizzand of Paris

Loose fitting raincoat in luxury Tergal—a fabric
that improves with washing. Decorative stitching
on fronts.

Rainwear, 2nd Floor.

September 20th to October 2nd

**Fashion Fortnight
at Peter Jones**

Sloane Square, S.W.1.
Sloane 3434

A Branch of the John Lewis Partnership

transistors **PHILIPS**

c'est plus sûr !

From the silk department, Miller had gone on to become a sports
buyer while doubling up as personal assistant to both Spedan Lewis and
Michael Watkins. He moved on swiftly in the 1930s to become financial
controller and a director of the company. He was very much a company man,
meeting his wife, Jessica, at John Lewis where she, too, worked as a buyer.
Two of their three sons became senior managers with the Partnership; the
third was a pilot.

Gathered around the new chairman were Spedan's 'bright young
things', now senior managers in the mid-1950s. Max Baker, a maths and
natural sciences graduate, had, after war service with the RAF, risen to
become Director of Selling and then Director of Trading. Paul May, who
started his career with John Lewis as a buyer of fancy silks, became Director
of Research and Expansion and, finally, from 1964, Director of Financial
Operations.

The third key member of Miller's team, however, was a very
different kettle of fish. Stanley Carter was to play a hugely important role
in the creation of Waitrose as we know it today. But what made Carter
so fascinating – and something of a legend in John Lewis history – is
that he came from a very different background from Spedan's Oxbridge
graduates, and behaved very differently, too. The son of an upholsterer
father and dressmaker mother, Carter joined John Lewis as a 16-year-old
school leaver in 1929. An RAF navigator during World War II, he was

Manufacturers
working
for
John Lewis

John Lewis has been manufacturing own-brand goods, formerly labelled 'Jonelle', for many decades (it was originally 'Jonell', the 'e' was added in the 1960s). This was not simply a case of quality control, but of ensuring reliable supplies of goods in times of economic and political uncertainty. Two London factories, the dressmaker C A Flawn and the bedding company Taylor & Penton founded in Chelsea by Spedan Lewis in 1935, found themselves exiled to the countryside during the Blitz. Charles Flawn had set up shop in Moorgate in 1900, yet for 20 years the factory was to be on St Ives' beautiful Porthmeor Beach, offering employment to young Cornish women at a time when traditional local jobs in pilchard fishing and tin mines were disappearing. A largely forgotten John Lewis outpost of the factory was sold to Berkertex of Bond Street in 1961. Packed off to Addlestone in Surrey, Taylor & Penton took root in the countryside, its workforce having to commute from their homes in Chelsea. Taylor & Penton went on to make duvets before these were fashionable in Britain, including one famous order for a Chelsea 'Madam's' poodle. The Addlestone factory was replaced in 1990 by purpose-built premises at nearby Brooklands, when this closed in 2001, another manufacturing unit that worked for John Lewis, Herbert Parkinson, took over some of the work.

appointed joint managing director of Oxford Street in 1958 with a brief to get the new store open and ready for business. His tenure lasted until 1966. Between 1960 and 1965, sales at Oxford Street very nearly doubled while profits rose fivefold. Before Carter – his fellow joint MD dealt with administration only – Oxford Street contributed 8 per cent of the Partnership's overall profit; by 1967, when he left to take over Waitrose, this figure had risen to 30 per cent.

Despite doing wonders for the newly rebuilt flagship store, Carter's controversial 'barrow boy' methods did not endear him to a polite and well-mannered staff who were used to highly civilized senior managers. He was a company man through and through, however – he liked to say that he wore a John Lewis badge on his pyjamas.

Miller decided to employ Carter's energy where it was needed most within the Partnership. This was Waitrose, a small chain of shops that had seemed all but irrelevant to the fortunes of the Partnership in the early 1950s. Not surprisingly, Carter's dynamism saw the number of Waitrose stores double during his six years as managing director. Sales rose threefold and profits by over 400 per cent.

On the technology front, John Lewis began using IBM mainframe computers at this time, mainly for stock control. John Lewis also invested significantly in design – especially in distinctive packaging for own-brand ranges that had become hallmarks of high quality and good value.

The value of the John Lewis buyers, meanwhile, remained as important as it had ever been under John Lewis himself. Miller, Carter and co. gave inspired buyers the independence to find out what customers might want and to source the best and most reliable suppliers. In fact, first-class relationships with suppliers were often down to the knowledge, good manners and sound business practices of men and women who travelled extensively. For them, many far-flung factories *were* 'John Lewis' and all that it represented.

One story fondly told in John Lewis circles concerns Peter Yaghmourian, the son of an Armenian immigrant and, in 1966, the stockings buyer at the Oxford Street store. That year, when Stanley Carter was still at Oxford Street, women's skirts rose thigh high and tights became instantly fashionable. Most English suppliers thought of the fashion for miniskirts, and thus tights, as a 'seven-day wonder', and so were unable to help Yaghmourian. Undaunted, he found a small supplier in Austria run by two concentration-camp survivors. They were delighted when Yaghmourian ordered 10,000 pairs. The tights sold out instantly, even though priced a little high, at 18s 11d a pair.

Lady Sieff, wife of a future chairman of Marks & Spencer, was one of those who rushed to buy pairs of the new tights at John Lewis. When she told her husband, Lord Sieff's M&S buyers offered the Austrians a much bigger order than Yaghmourian's. But, because they got on so well with the John Lewis buyer, and liked the idea of the Partnership, they held their course. They told the M&S buyers that they had enough money and would not be able to supply a rival. In fact, they were able to increase supply, allowing the price of tights on sale in Oxford Street to fall to 9s 11d a pair.

It is significant that, despite retirements and the lure of other jobs in rival firms, more than half of John Lewis's buyers in 1972, as Bernard

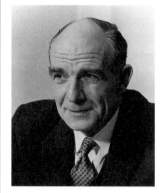

Senior Partners of the Consumer Boom:

Top
Max Baker, Director of Trading.

Centre
Paul May, Director of Financial Operations.

Bottom
Stanley Carter, Managing Director, Waitrose.

Roy Jenkins, at 11 Downing Street as
Chancellor of the Exchequer in 1970 (above).
When he left Downing Street, his furniture was
moved out by John Lewis Removals (below).

A design for the interior
of John Lewis Oxford Street
by Raymond Loewy's studio, 1960.

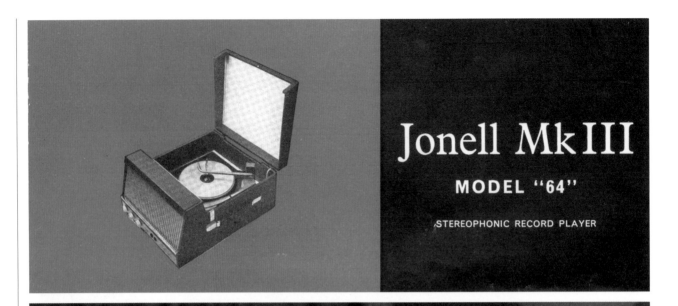

Jonell Mk III

MODEL "64"

STEREOPHONIC RECORD PLAYER

Miller retired, had been with the Partnership since 1955. Good working conditions had certainly encouraged staff to stay on for the long term.

In London, to celebrate the centenary of the firm in 1964, Miller had commissioned Barbara Hepworth's Oxford Street sculpture in 1961, a commitment to modern art to go with the chairman's belief in good design. Indeed, between 1957 and 1966 he was a member of the Council of Industrial Design, the precursor to the Design Council of today, whose purpose was to promote good design in the products of British industry.

At the time of the John Lewis centenary, Miller stated that the Partnership 'manages to preserve its innate character while keeping abreast of the fast-moving needs of social change'. He left the Partnership in fine shape when he retired. He enjoyed a second career as the Treasurer and Pro-Chancellor of Southampton University before finally retiring at the age of 87 in 1991. Bernard Miller died in 2003 and, during his impressive chairmanship, it might be said that the John Lewis Partnership had never had it so good.

DESIGN

John Lewis had long demonstrated its interest in design through its links to smaller manufacturing and the modern design of its buildings. With the appointment of Robin and Lucienne Day as official design consultants in 1962, good design became a central part of the company ethic.

As a profession, design emerged comparatively recently in Britain, roughly from the 1920s onwards, and really took off only after the opening of the Festival of Britain on London's South Bank in 1951. Its strikingly modern pavilions were clustered around the brand-new Royal Festival Hall. The festival was a great success and attracted over 8 million visitors. Its popularity was in large part because it was entertaining as well as instructive. It did not preach the message of 'good design'; rather, it let people *enjoy* contemporary design.

This spirit had long pervaded John Lewis stores up and down the country. Indeed, it stretches all the way back to its historic roots in manufacturing textiles and fabrics, including its purchase of Herbert Parkinson in 1953 and the rich and varied designs it acquired when it bought the Stead McAlpin factory near Carlisle in 1965. This became a base for the production of its own designs by Cavendish Textiles. The rebuilding of the Peter Jones store in the 1930s along Modernist lines showed not only that John Lewis saw the value of good design early on but also how far in advance of its peers it has been in this area.

Below
Cavendish Textiles was based in London and began in 1930, when it was known as the Cavendish Buying Agency. Below is the Daisy Chain textile manufactured by Cavendish between 1965 and 1989 and re-created for the 150 Years Anniversary and, bottom, an original Cavendish fabric.

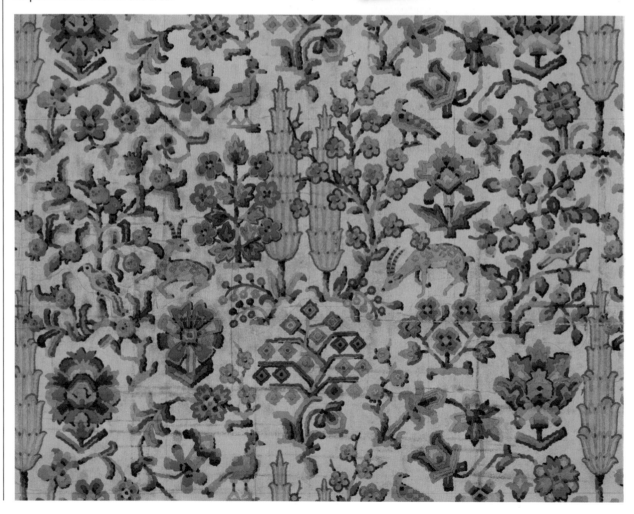

1956
Vitra Eames lounge armchair by Charles and Ray Eames for Herman Miller.

1962
Flos Arco lamp by Achille and Pier Giacomo Castiglioni.

1969
Kartell Componibili circular storage unit by Anna Castelli for Kartell.

1956
Vitra Yanagi Butterfly stool by Sori Yanagi for Tendo Mokko.

1944
Vitra Noguchi coffee table by Isamu Noguchi for Herman Miller.

Above
Robin and Lucienne Day in 1979.

Right
Lucienne Day fabric samples for John Lewis.

Opposite
Lucienne Day inspecting a Thai and Indian 'silk mosaic' in the cafe of John Lewis Kingston upon Thames, 1990.

Aside from increasing the popularity of design, the Festival of Britain also prompted companies to develop what would now be called a 'corporate identity', whereby a consistent approach to design would run through every aspect of a company – from letterheads to uniforms and delivery vans. Companies began to realize that consistent and easily recognized corporate identities were good for business. A newly mobile and more affluent population might respond favourably through their purses and wallets, if they were able to recognize a trusted and favourite store as they drove from town to town. At John Lewis this new focus on design was marked particularly by Max Baker, John Lewis's Director of Selling, hiring the gifted husband-and-wife team Robin and Lucienne Day as design consultants in 1962. Robin Day had designed all the seating at the Royal Festival Hall, a commission that made his name in the public eye.

He met Lucienne Conradi, a talented textile student, at a Royal College of Art dance in 1940, and in 1942 they were married. A decade later, they had become the golden couple of British design.

Before the Days came on board in 1962 there was no consistent approach to design at John Lewis. In the teeth of increasing competition, it seemed to the Days – and, at first, to Max Baker – that there was no time to lose in the creation of a 'corporate identity' that would make what we would today call the John Lewis 'brand' as strong as that of London Transport, Shell or Penguin Books.

The Partnership had dipped a toe in the waters of various forms of corporate identity in the 1950s, with, for example, some exemplary new packaging by Jesse Collins, who had established Britain's first graphic design department at the Central School of Arts and Crafts in

1945. It had also worked with individual designers, such as the renowned American industrial studio of Raymond Loewy. However, what the Days proposed, and Bernard Miller and his fellow directors now agreed to, was nothing less than a comprehensive 'makeover' of the Partnership's image.

The Days suggested that they write a report on what needed to be done. Completed the following year, their analysis seems a modest effort by today's standards. A simple typed document with no illustrations, glossy or otherwise, it was a matter-of-fact and extremely thoughtful view of what might be achieved. Their report covered everything from architecture, signage, interiors, display and packaging to stationery, transport, publicity and publications.

They were faced with what proved to be a huge task that took many years to put into practice. Yet, as Robin Day said, 'we were so deep into the Partnership and so much liked the people we met, that we felt a part of it. There was no question of giving it up.'

The Days' role as design consultants involved recommending, vetting and briefing designers brought into the John Lewis fold. Robin went on to design the interiors of a number of John Lewis and Waitrose stores (notably the Milton Keynes branches of both, opened in 1979), while Lucienne produced a range of furnishing fabrics for John Lewis in 1973–74 before she turned to the design of her remarkable and ambitious 'silk mosaics'. (She had designed dress fabrics for John Lewis in the 1950s.) Like giant tapestries, the silk mosaics were made from hundreds, and even many thousands, of pieces of Thai and Indian silk. One of the best known is the shimmering *Aspects of the Sun*, hanging in the coffee shop of John Lewis Kingston upon Thames, which opened in 1990.

One of the Days' most important appointments came in 1964 when they commissioned Hans Schleger to help them create the new corporate identity. Schleger (1898–1976), often known by his pseudonym, 'Zero', was a German designer who had helped establish professional modern design in Britain.

Schleger's initial recommendation was for Helvetica, a Swiss sans-serif (plain) typeface developed from 1957, to be used for all Partnership display type and lettering – whether on shopfronts, delivery vans, advertising or letterheads. He believed that Helvetica reflected 'the straightforwardness, honesty, clarity and wholesomeness' of the Partnership. John Lewis was thus an early convert to this enduring font, a design policy put into practice by Peter Hatch, a graphic designer who also created new, abstract Op Art-style carrier bags. At the beginning of the twenty-first century John Lewis turned to Gill Sans, a far more distinctive typeface than the now near-ubiquitous Helvetica.

Schleger also designed the famous John Lewis Partnerhip logo, a loop and twist of the three letters, and, together with the Days, agreed on green as the principal colour for its corporate identity. Company legend has it that this was inspired by the green ink that Spedan Lewis had used exclusively to write his many memos, as had later chairmen. And, today, because our high streets and roads are saturated in dazzling colour, the dark green – and crisp modern lettering – of John Lewis delivery vans and lorries stands, out from the crowd.

The Days' aim was to pull the Partnership together visually. This meant bringing John Lewis shops, still sporting their original names, into one corporate fold. In their 1963 report, they wrote:

Although existing buildings must remain, any new exterior lettering is being done in a new standard form. Standard treatment of interior signs and lettering is also helping towards the clarity, order and simplicity which is our aim. The packaging of a great variety of John Lewis Partnership merchandise has been redesigned in a distinctive modern and related style. Planned colour schemes

Above left
Hans 'Zero' Schleger.

Above middle
Schleger's original sketch for the John Lewis Partnership logo: 'A symbol that would express something of the special unifying character of the Partnership' as *The Gazette* described it.

Above right
Schleger's redesign of the John Lewis Partnership logo, 1964.

Below
Jonelle packaging from the 1960s, with its Op Art-style pattern.

John Lewis Op Art-style
carrier bags from 1968.

have been introduced for offices and all non-selling areas, stationery redesigned and a new livery for all vehicles introduced. Certain visual elements have been agreed on and are applied wherever possible to strengthen the house style and the link between the branches. These are the colours dark green with white, and sometimes a light green accent, a Partnership symbol, and the use of a particular type of lettering. Almost before anything else, we must, in designing the Partnership, avoid fussiness and we must work towards order, clarity and a modernity that will not tire.

An internal design committee was set up in 1965 to keep tabs on the implementation of the new corporate identity. To make this formidable task easier, two years later the Days produced a comprehensive *John Lewis Partnership Design Manual*. This was followed by the creation of an in-house design department. The Days chose Graham Heywood, followed by Douglas Cooper, the Partnership's design coordinator from 1979 until his retirement in 2002. 'We co-operated fully with him', said Lucienne of Heywood, 'and watched the development of the department with great satisfaction.'

For his part, Douglas Cooper intuitively understood that the Partnership's design had to be crisp, clear, fresh and enduring at one and the same time. In a world of increasingly frantic change, this was always a tall order. And

Above
Stylish 1960s exhibitions of commercial, retail and industrial design at London's instructive and popular Design Centre.

Opposite
John Lewis furniture department, 1970, featuring Eero Saarinen's Tulip chair (below in a modern reproduction).

Circular Table
WITH WHITE FORMICA
42 inches
£34.00

£46.00

Oliver Hrubiak
Finn chair

Leonhard Pfeifer
Abbeywood cabinet

Wales & Wales
Radar dining table

Sitting Firm
Glenmore rocking chair

Margo Selby
Brighton cushion

Bethan Gray
Noah bench

Ebbe Gehl
Mira bookcase

Timorous Beasties
Waxwing Bird cushion

yet, he was able to achieve this balance even in the design of carrier bags. In 1989, Cooper commissioned a new bag from the design consultancy Lloyd Northover. The aim for the design was to make it feel as if it had been there all the time, and for it to last for the next 25 years. With a few tweaks, it has.

Meanwhile, John McConnell of Pentagram – the man behind the graphic image of Biba, the 1960s London fashion boutique – brought John Lewis's corporate image up to date again from 2003. The belief at John Lewis is that although change is often necessary in the rapidly moving retail world, it should seem natural, the right thing to do. Through the pages of *The Gazette*, individual Partners have been able to express their own views on new design initiatives; as in the past, they have not always been complimentary – especially if they have suspected change merely for change's sake.

Design that comes and goes like the tide is unlikely to win loyalty or long-term customers, and so change at John Lewis has been evolutionary. This fundamental grasp of what makes lasting quality in design has been reflected in the changing nature of goods on offer in John Lewis stores. Where customers can still find rolls of cottons and silks, and upholstered armchairs; they can also choose from the latest designs from Design Icons, original design classics by renowned designers, or John Lewis Design Collective, a range of new products that are the result of exclusive collaborations with established and emerging designers. This latter includes living- and dining-room furniture by Matthew Hilton, barware by Nick Munro, cabinets by Leonhard Pfeifer, furniture by Ebbe Gehl and cushions by Bluebellgray. The Scottish design duo Timorous Beasties has created a range of extraordinary cushions using digital techniques.

Where design was once more about manufacturing and the individual product, today it's more about 'lifestyle' and choice. John Lewis is one of the biggest names in the home market, and so what the company does helps to shape people's homes; it's not something superficial, something just to be applied.

John Lewis has also developed an extensive range of own-brand fashion collections. These are a close collaboration between buyers and designers, with teams working together far in advance on ideas for trends and colours. In 2012 a new fashion line, Somerset, designed by Alice Temperley, was launched to great acclaim and became the fastest-selling collection in John Lewis's history. The Kin range, launched in 2013, was the first time that John Lewis had produced a collection that spanned menswear, womenswear and childrenswear, the whole range having a clean, modern and Scandinavian-inspired aesthetic. John Lewis commissioned the graphic designer Mark Farrow to ensure that the branding reflected the ethos and look of the range.

To help encourage future generations of designers, John Lewis works with students at Central Saint Martins College of Art and Design, Glasgow School of Art and the Royal College of Art. The company also sponsors the Elle Decoration British Design Awards. In 2012 it launched its New Designers award to find new designers.

5

NEW
BUSINESS
METHODS

1972–2000

In the first weeks of 1972 the miners went on strike. The Conservative government, led by Edward Heath, declared a state of emergency. Unemployment soared, reaching a million for the first time since the 1930s. The school-leaving age was raised to 16, yet still the number on the dole rose. The dockers went on strike in July. In 1973 the Oil Crisis would hit home and the country would be plunged into a three-day week and electricity rationing. At the beginning of that year, Britain had joined the European Common Market (today's EU).

In the 1970s the country creaked and groaned from an era of industrial strife, British-built cars and holidays at home, to a very different society, which in some ways really did become increasingly 'middle class'. There was a widespread desire for 'sophistication', although it would take another decade before 'good design' became part of British social aspirations. People were more affluent, discriminating and aware of what was on offer – whether in food, fashion and furniture or education, culture and travel. This was reflected in the healthy expansion of John Lewis throughout the decade despite the grim economic conditions that characterized much of the period.

Small ads in *The Gazette* are a telling guide to social change in the 1970s, and to Britain's rising middle-class ambitions. In October 1972 – as Peter Lewis took over from Bernard Miller as chairman of the John Lewis Partnership, and a Furnishing Fabrics Manager at Oxford Street earned £2,750 a year – there were ads for an Austin A40 with 31,000 miles on the clock for £175. Someone in West Hampstead was offering 60p an hour for a cleaner, and there were English seaside cottages to rent. In 1982, the ads were for second-hand Citroëns and Datsuns, and holiday lets in Torremolinos. In 1991, it was Volvos and BMWs, and timeshares in Florida.

Through all these changes, the tall, elegant and patrician figure of Peter Lewis stood unflinching at the helm. He had been called to the Bar in 1956, and yet – three years later, and much to the initial dismay of his father, Oswald Lewis – Peter joined the Partnership as a management trainee. Although a grandson of the founder, he could expect no special treatment: Spedan Lewis had made sure of that. Peter, though, rose quickly through

Opposite
Early VDU screens in use in an office at Stevenage: this period was to see the rise and dominance of the desktop computer.

Above
Peter Lewis (seated left) takes on the chairmanship from Bernard Miller (seated right) in 1972.

A 'Continental Evening' at the John Barnes Social Club in August 1974 introduces Partners to the pleasures of Yugoslavian wine and Hungarian salami.

the Partnership ranks. By the end of his first year, he was managing the stationery department at Oxford Street. He was soon a buyer, and, by 1967, Director of Trading. Clear, direct, questioning, impeccably mannered and commanding, Peter was a natural successor to Bernard Miller. He proved to be an excellent choice as the Partnership's chairman from 1972 to 1992.

Despite a bleak economic backdrop, soaring inflation, pay restrictions, the threat – real and hoax – of IRA bombs in central London, and waves of intense industrial strife, the company's selling space doubled in those 20 years. John Lewis stores opened in Scotland. There was the first out-of-town branch, in the new Brent Cross shopping centre in north London. Truly ambitious new John Lewis stores like the riverside Kingston upon Thames branch took a full 20 years to plan, design and build, with the first store having both a John Lewis and a Waitrose. It took another six years to rebuild Heelas of Reading, with the amalgamation of several shops into one. Such projects would not be undertaken lightly in boom years, let alone the 1970s. But, as Peter Lewis said, 'Our calculations are for 25 years, but our hopes are set on a hundred.'

Significantly, however, Ian Anderson, brought on board in 1977 as Director of Trading (or Managing Director, in today's terms), was a buyer who had become expert in computing. In fact, Anderson played a key role in the development of EPOS, or 'electronic point of sale', systems, in British retailing. Now, for the first time, tills registered the sale of

Classified ads and the Partners's diary from the back page of *The Gazette*, 29 May 1965.

Orange was one of the inescapable colours of the 1970s: this is lunchtime at the restaurant in the brand-new John Lewis Edinburgh in the brutalist St James Shopping Centre, 1973.

goods electronically, with information passed on to stock controllers in warehouses. The first such system to be installed at John Lewis was in the Oxford Street hardware department in 1970.

Anderson's most radical scheme, however, was for a 'furnishing and leisure' warehouse-style shop alongside the new M40 motorway outside High Wycombe, Buckinghamshire. The building was a glorified warehouse, and there was a feeling among many in John Lewis that a lack of the sheer assortment of goods that customers had come to expect would lead to poor trading. Far from it, however. Highly visible from the motorway, the warehouse store drew in so many customers that, very soon, this rather quiet and leisurely stretch of road became gridlocked!

Peter Lewis believed that the John Lewis Partnership had a duty to take the long-term view. As he told the Partnership Council in 1973, he felt it best not to be drawn into what he described as the 'whirlpool' of advertising, credit cards, trading stamps and other 'experiments', which might be short-lived or, at the very least, needed to be proved worthwhile over the long haul.

While happy to go along with the Equal Pay Act of 1975, the metrication of fabric lengths and computerization, the Partnership management team remained suspicious of the merits not only of advertising, but also – and especially – of Sunday trading. Boring British Sundays had been lampooned for some years; Tony Hancock's *A Sunday*

TEASMADE

... A NEW SERVICE
by
GOBLIN

Charming, handy and somehow always rather comical, the bedside Goblin Teasmade has been a staple of British domestic life since it first went on sale in 1936. There had been Heath Robinson-style Victorian devices powered by gas since the early 1890s, but the electric Teasmade, invented by William Hermann Brenner Thornton, complete with reading light and alarm clock, was safe and effectively foolproof. The alarm clock switched on an electric element that boiled water in the kettle; it was then piped by a tube to the teapot. The whole caboodle switched itself off. Production was halted during World War II – a Teasmade was deemed an unnecessary luxury – but resumed in 1947.

The Teasmade's heyday was undoubtedly the 1960s and 1970s, when you could buy models framing your favourite photographs; later sales began to slump. Today, however, the Teasmade, owned by Swan since the early 1980s, is enjoying something of a revival. The latest models boast AM/FM radios as well as alarm clocks and reading lamps. They might seem eccentric and redolent of the most suburban ways of life, yet here is a design that has touched the heart of the nation and served it its favourite beverage for three-quarters of a century.

c.1902
Automatic tea-making machine.

1972
Vintage Goblin 860 Teasmade.

2014
Swan Teasmade.

Afternoon at Home for the BBC Home Service, broadcast in 1958, caught the public mood brilliantly. However, Peter Lewis believed firmly in the idea of a day of rest, and this included a break from commerce and shopping. He was to be a keen supporter of the Keep Sunday Special Campaign, founded in 1985.

Nothing, though, could convince the post-1970s British public that shopping was not the be-all and end-all of life. In 1994, a Conservative government under John Major enacted the Sunday Trading Act, allowing large stores to open for up to six hours on Sundays. The Partnership fell into line. And, now, with Stuart Hampson as chairman, it began to advertise. In 1995, it even appointed a public relations officer from outside the company. This was Helen Dickinson, a former TV documentary maker, who found herself at the sharp end of the Partnership's reluctance over advertising. One John Lewis buyer flatly informed her: 'I will not be forced into promoting my products.' One retired Partner wrote to *The Gazette* regarding advertising campaigns that had been long months in the making, 'I must confess that my opinion of most people in the ad industry is of con-men'.

Peter Lewis himself had said in a speech to the Partnership's Central Council in 1986:

> I need not remind you because you know very well that the Partnership does not believe that the larger the better, or the faster the growth the better either, for the true health of the business or for the comfort of our customers. Our ambition is not size, but quality.

Partly because the Partnership advertised so little, the point of sale was, according to Douglas Cooper, who was in charge of corporate design, 'the moment of truth for customers'. This encouraged Cooper and his team to aim for the very highest, and most consistent, standards of design throughout the Partnership. It led to awards for the design of food packaging, carrier bags and corporate colour schemes. As the design industry itself boomed from the early 1980s, John Lewis shops focused increasingly on the design of goods, and so there was a steady upward spiral in standards.

This was achieved by adhering to the high standards of Brian O'Callaghan, John Lewis's Director of Trading from 1990 to 2000, who had been director of selling from the mid-1980s. Good design was important, but could not be displayed without maintaining rigorous shop keeping standards. O'Callaghan was keen to keep the Partnership in touch with new trends and under his watchful eye the business adopted changes that fitted the John Lewis model of clean lines, modesty and good taste.

Even then, however, some were suspicious of the changes. 'What fantastic brains they must have to come up with this rubbish', wrote one Partner to *The Gazette* after the 1989 corporate design makeover by Lloyd Northover. And, when the Boilerhouse Project – precursor of the Design Museum – opened in 1981 in the Victoria and Albert Museum in South Kensington, John Lewis was on its guard. *The Gazette* asked June Fraser, its Head of Graphics, to review the opening exhibition. Fraser, suspicious of the view that industrially produced products could somehow be the equivalent of Art, wrote:

Above
Labour Party leader Neil Kinnock lending support to the 'Keep Sunday Special Campaign', launched in 1985; from 1994, department stores were allowed to open for six hours on Sundays.

Opposite
One of many new electronic goods marketed by John Lewis in the 1970s was the Atari video games console, at play here in an archetypal 1970s living room.

Above
Exhibition of Olivetti design at the
Boilerhouse Project, forerunner of the Design
Museum, at the Victoria and Albert Museum,
opened in 1981.

The difficulty is that design has to be experienced. Although its artefacts are
an accurate reflection of man's progress, it is not 'culture'; it should not be a
part of a museum, or put on a pedestal, or behind a Perspex case. Design is
part of everyday living, a three-dimensional experience. Perhaps subsequent
exhibitions [on Sony and Braun] will be more relevant to real people.

At the time, John Lewis created products with the simplest labels,
which were well designed but functionally so. And, although more emphasis
than ever before had been given to fashion in John Lewis stores, there
was a lingering – perhaps intentional – sense of 1950s, or even pre-war,
taste about some of the clothes and fabrics on display at Oxford Street and
elsewhere. At the start of the 1980s, UK cinemas were screening *The Mirror*
Crack'd, an Agatha Christie 'Miss Marple' film starring Angela Lansbury. The
story was set in 1953, and Jonelle Duracolour wallpapers were chosen for
the elderly-spinster protagonist's home.

Design, however, took off in the 1980s, and, as John Lewis opened
in Aberdeen in 1989, Oxford Street began stocking expensive 'designer'
kettles, notably a pair of Alessi models by Richard Sapper and Michael
Graves. These featured American train-whistle and whistling-bird chimes
as water came to the boil. Design not only represented modern culture, but
quite soon, was synonymous with it.

Despite so much expansion and thoughtful modernization, the
Partnership was often regarded as quirky and even eccentric. This was
unfair, although Stuart Hampson, looking back in 1998 over his first five
years as chairman, said that John Lewis had opened up and was shedding
its 'Trappist tendencies'. In other words, an inward-looking organization
was looking out to the world. This tendency had, again, been reflected in
the lively pages of *The Gazette*, edited in the Hampson era by Penny Junor,
a well-respected Fleet Street and *Private Eye* journalist. Trips were made on

behalf of *The Gazette* to department stores in continental Europe, like Stockmann's of Helsinki, that had something of the same ethos as John Lewis.

Stuart Hampson, a former civil servant, had joined the Partnership in 1982. He was Managing Director of Tyrrell & Green (now John Lewis), Southampton, before being appointed to the board in 1986 as Director of Research and Expansion. During his chairmanship, John Lewis expanded with new stores, notably in central Glasgow and a high-profile branch in the huge Bluewater shopping mall in north Kent.

Against a backdrop of expansion and a short-lived economic boom, the belief was encouraged that every business could be privatized to advantage. The resulting business atmosphere led to one real crisis, and test of strength, for the Partnership. This was a disorganized and unfocused campaign, among what proved to be a minority of Partners, to float the Partnership on the Stock Exchange. The driving force was less political than a belief that if the Partnership could be sold, then every Partner would stand to gain £100,000.

Hampson launched a counter-attack. The Partnership, he said loudly and clearly in 1999, was not for sale. It was owned by a trust, and 'Spedan took great care in the way he set up the Trust to ensure that the gift of his business would be enjoyed by successive generations of Partners and couldn't be hijacked once he had disappeared from the scene'. The only certainty the recently knighted chairman could foresee if the campaign continued was divisive debate. The debate was certainly heated, and it took some years before the majority of Partners were convinced that the organization's business model did not need 'fixing'. It already gave them a degree of ownership impossible in a conventional private company, a camaraderie, a social life and economic security during pressured times.

This real sense of security began to seem ever more important as John Lewis faced up to a new world of Internet shopping, instant and global electronic communications, and ever-fiercer competition. The Partnership had expanded and had taken calculated risks from 1972 to the turn of the millennium. However, by growing carefully and thoughtfully it avoided many of the perils faced by rival companies dedicated to serving shareholders and prey to takeovers and other financial uncertainties. In fact, it was the John Lewis model of ownership and control that began to be praised increasingly by central government from the start of the new century.

In 1995, the Partnership buried a 50-year time capsule at Cheadle. One of Penny Junor's predictions for 2045 was that we might all have computers in our homes and would communicate through the Internet. That was to happen within five years. But the menu proposed for the 2045 John Lewis Central Council dinner sounded quirkily interesting: smoked tuna and kelp mousse served with lemon mayonnaise followed by roast ostrich in 'nil calorific' gravy with mixed organic vegetables, and a platter of Amazonian fruits. What is certain is that by the end of the millennium, John Lewis had come a very long way from just a quarter of a century earlier. Then, Central Council and other meetings had been held under 'Gaz' lamps and strings of naked light bulbs connected up to emergency generators, as industrial strife plunged the country into darkness. By the year 2000 things seemed a lot brighter.

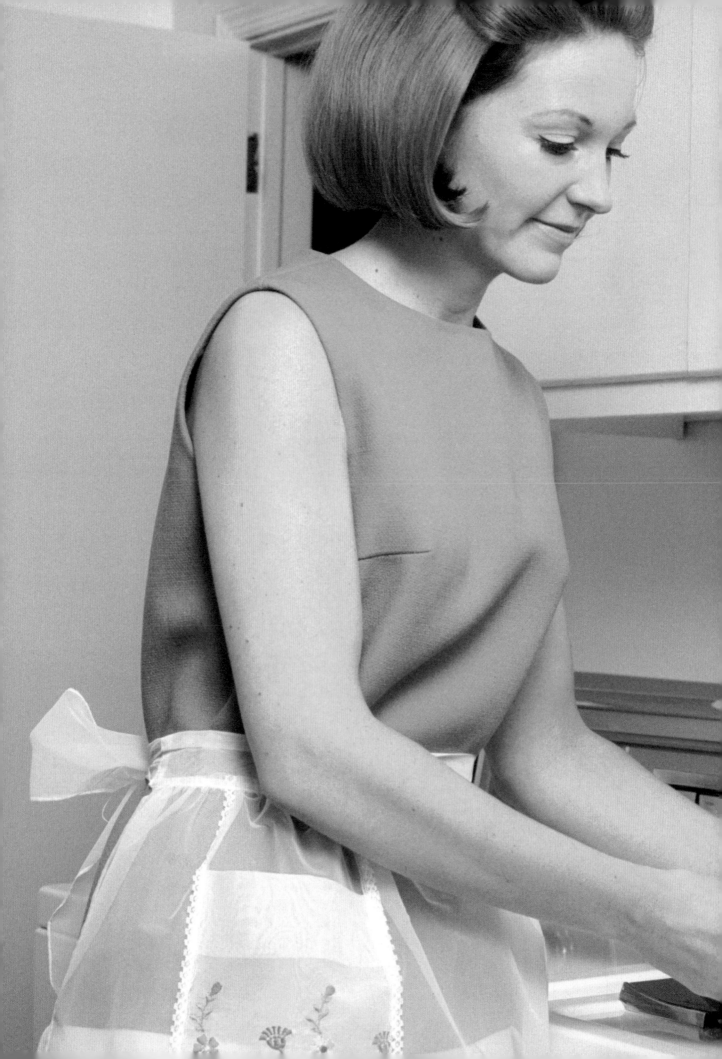

HOUSEHOLD
PRODUCTS

&

EVERYDAY
LIFE

From 1955, the British consumer economy boomed with a very loud
bang. Ever since, the country has been a nation of passionate shoppers
as well as shopkeepers, and with a changing selection of alluring
goods that meet the changing ways of life.

1953
Grundig television console.

1954
Murphy 14-inch V240 TV set.

The first ever British television advert, broadcast on 22 September 1955, was for Gibbs SR toothpaste. That evening, 658,000 viewers gawping at the screens of 122,000 'goggle boxes', mainly in and around London, watched 23 adverts in all for consumer goods ranging from Cadbury's milk chocolate to Esso petrol. A number of politicians, academics, critics and concerned middle-class parents believed the advent of television advertising to be the beginning of a moral decline. Lord Reith, the formidable Director-General of the BBC, was still unrepentant years later. On the BBC's *Face to Face* programme in 1960, he told his interviewer that the ending of the corporation's monopoly in broadcasting had been 'one of the most deplorable mistakes ever made in public affairs'.

The majority of the public, however, simply wanted to shop, and they lapped up TV advertising. Rationing, slowly phased out after World War II, was finally repealed in July 1954. Unemployment and inflation were low, yet wages were rising along with social and material ambitions. Britain and Europe were enjoying what was to be a long spell of peace and prosperity.

TVs themselves were one of the most popular new consumer goods. Enormous, heavy and often unreliable, these 'television sets' were mostly rented by British households: it was cheaper because weekly rental fees included service and repairs.

Rental and hire purchase, which also enabled many parents to buy school uniforms and children's clothes, were now part of life for millions of British families whose desire for better and newer things easily outstripped their incomes. This was an age before credit cards, easily arranged bank loans and, indeed, bank accounts; the majority of the working population was still paid in cash. Overdrafts were scarce and holidays abroad remained the stuff of glossy-brochure fantasies. Bit by bit, however, households across

c.1970
Sony Trinitron
colour television receiver.

2014
John Lewis JL9000 Smart TV.

Opposite
The very first advert on British television, in 1955, was for Gibbs SR toothpaste, when the design of TV cabinets was influenced more by timber than by technology.

the social spectrum began to invest in the kind of domestic products that North Americans had been familiar with since the 1930s. Among these were washing machines, electric radios and record players – and, for the better off, juicers and radiograms.

The shelves of John Lewis stores groaned under the weight of these costly and heavily advertised machines. Vacuum cleaners, fridges and blenders had been around in the US for decades. To UK consumers, however, they marked a minor revolution, spelling the end of an essentially Victorian Britain, still characterized by coal-burning stoves, outdoor lavatories and larders (rather than refrigerators).

For most families except the poorest, real change came in the 1960s as the price of household goods fell. There were many reasons for this. One was the abolition, in 1964, of something known as Resale Price Maintenance. This had prevented shops from discounting goods, so whether you bought your huge new timber-framed television set from John Lewis or your local electrical supplier, the price would, by law, have been the same. At John Lewis, fair prices were underpinned by the company's Never Knowingly Undersold commitment.

Automatic washing machines, like this 1947 Thor model from Chicago, were a long time coming to Britain; this one even doubled up as a dishwasher.

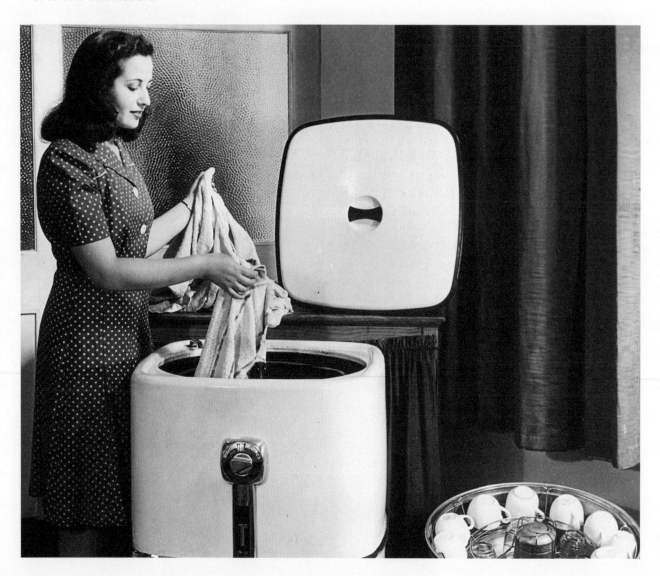

1897
Vowel Y hand-cranked
washing machine by Thomas
Bradford.

early mid-20th century
Ceramic washing tub with
attached wringer.

1963
John Bloom's Rolls
Duo-matic twin-tub.

2014
John Lewis JLWM1411
washing machine.

1934
Xavier Pauchard
Tolix 'A' chair.

1950
Charles and Ray Eames
DSW Side Chair.

1960
Verner Panton
S chair.

1977
Hans Wegner
Butterfly easy chair.

2000
Jasper Morrison
Magis Air chair.

2000
Shin and Tomoko Azumi
Lem bar stool.

2002
Philippe Starck
Louis Ghost chair.

2009
Philippe Stark
Masters chair.

2011
Edward Barber & Jay Osgerby
Tip Ton chair.

Opposite
Original classic chair designs
stocked as part of the current
John Lewis range.

Right
A hit from 1963, the
psychedelic Astro lava lamp.

Another explanation for falling prices was the popular advent of cheap and cheery materials like plastic, polythene, plywood, nylon, rayon and fibreglass. These had all been around for some time, but lowered manufacturing costs meant that they could now be used in the production of cheap domestic goods – from cups and school lunch boxes to dustpans and brushes, furniture and fabrics.

Plastic and other synthetic materials were also used to make colourful, adventurous and playful products and artworks. And there were brilliantly designed objects, too, that were both timelessly functional and in tune with the spirit of the age. Joe Colombo's Universale plastic chair for Kartell is a classic example – as, of course, is the multi-million-selling Polypropylene chair for Hille designed by Robin Day in 1963.

Pop culture led to a flurry of comic-book-style objects for the home. None, perhaps, was more characteristic of the era than the psychedelic Astro lava lamp. Invented in 1963 – the year of Beatlemania – by Edward Craven-Walker, the lava lamp was a sensation. Blobs of coloured wax were heated by a light bulb inside a glass lamp filled with clear liquid. As they warmed up, the blobs began to stretch and distort, creating hypnotic plays and ever-shifting shapes. Today, the lamps are still very much in production – and can be bought from John Lewis.

But, while the trend for exciting new designs and materials undoubtedly accelerated through the 1960s, there remained high demand for traditional household goods – from curtains and furnishing fabrics to tea towels and cotton sheets. And, in these areas, John Lewis met demand and thrived. Its well-known Jonelle trademark, founded in 1937, remained a hallmark of good-quality essential design until 2003 when the 'John Lewis' brand replaced it. John Lewis was, in fact, the most active of the major UK retailers in the design and manufacture of modern textiles; even in the 1960s it continued to sell an extraordinary range of fabrics, from the traditional to the avant-garde. Pat Albeck's Daisy Chain, for example, proved a top-selling fabric year after year, it was a popular choice for bed linen and tea towels. At this time, John Lewis was printing its own textiles at the Stead McAlpin factory in Carlisle and at Herbert Parkinson; John Lewis had, in 1965, taken control of this proud Victorian company – Queen Victoria herself had been a loyal customer – in order to ensure a continued supply of the best British textiles.

Also at this time, John Lewis was manufacturing furniture for kitchens, bedrooms and living rooms. In fact, the sheer variety of its products was extraordinary – especially considering the growing fame of individual designers and companies devoted to the making and marketing of self-consciously 'designed' goods. While

The apotheosis of 1980s 'designer' culture: (left) the Juicy Salif lemon squeezer by Phillipe Starck and (left below) a stainless-steel kettle of 1985, complete with whistling bird, by Michael Graves, a Postmodern American architect, for Alessi.

John Lewis was quick to stock and sell the latest and best-value household goods from other manufacturers, its own-brand products continued to thrive, being well made and designed, as well as good value.

It is remarkable how Jonelle products are traded on eBay – whether fabrics, curtains, cushions or even record players. It was this sheer variety of own-brand goods that made John Lewis so different, and this remains true even today. While some major retailers have abandoned their own in-house goods, John Lewis's products have gone from strength to strength, and, in recent years, have been sold under a bright, clear, attractive and, most importantly, unapologetic 'John Lewis' label.

Increasingly, though, the names of particular designers and specific manufacturers of household goods began to matter, especially in the 1980s – the 'Designer Decade' – as consumers became more prosperous and, perhaps, more discerning. Advertising budgets were also cranked up, to create 'brands'. This meant that shoppers began to look out for lamps and chairs, hairdryers and lemon squeezers, and, eventually even vacuum cleaners, designed by recognizable 'names'.

The choice of the last-named pair is no coincidence: the lemon squeezer *par excellence* was the Juicy Salif, a playful kitchen product by the provocative French designer Philippe Starck. When it went on sale in 1990, it caused a sensation in culinary and design circles. Given that you could buy a perfectly decent lemon squeezer for ten times less, who on earth would splash out on such a costly 'designer' object? But, that was precisely the point. A new generation, brought up with a taste for self-conscious design, proved perfectly willing to spend good money on a kitchen gadget, like the Alessi kettle, that is also a work of eye-catching domestic sculpture. It has been in production ever since – and stocked, of course, by John Lewis.

As for vacuum cleaners . . . even when these were well designed, as Hoovers and many others had been for several decades, they were hidden away in understairs cupboards. All this changed when, in the 1990s, James Dyson, a British inventor, launched his Dual Cyclone vacuum cleaner. This powerful cyclonic cleaner did away with the need for dust bags inside the machine. Aside from its powerful performance, the Dyson cleaner was clearly the work of an individual. It was brightly coloured, and designed to be looked at. Since the success of the Dual Cyclone, ever more household objects have been designed as colourful, characterful artefacts that, however humble or basic, look good once their task is completed.

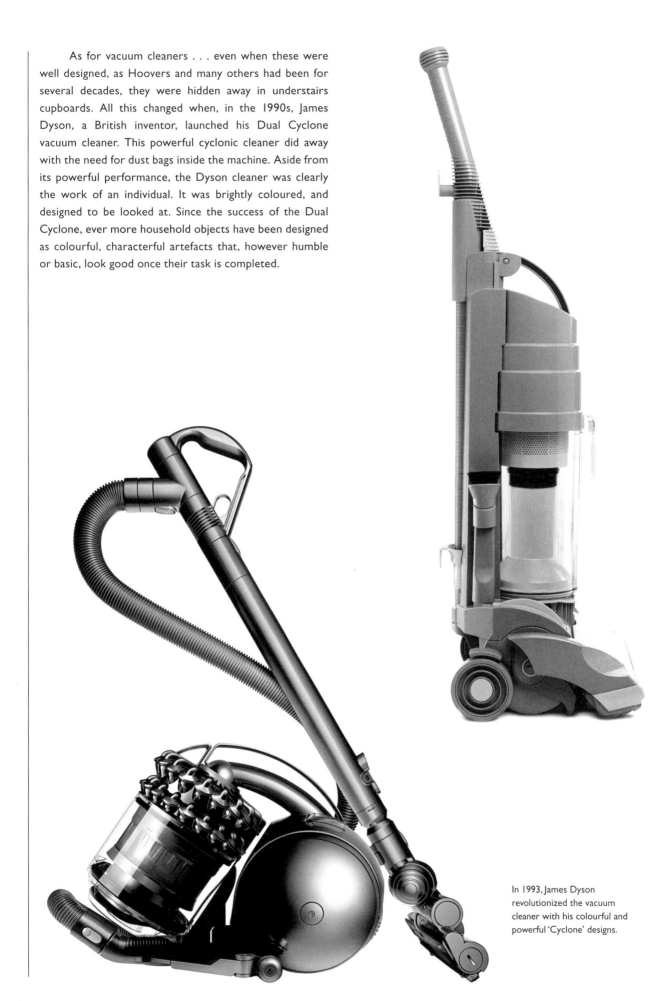

In 1993, James Dyson revolutionized the vacuum cleaner with his colourful and powerful 'Cyclone' designs.

TEA FOR TWO

This page shows brands of teapot that John Lewis has stocked in the past. The opposite page shows teapots from the company's current range.

1800s
Nineteenth-century teapot with Egyptian motifs by Josiah Wedgwood.

1920
Salt-glazed stoneware teapot designed by Lambeth Art Pottery, manufactured by Doulton & Co.

1935
Porcelain teapot painted in orange and lustre by Wedgwood.

1940s
Large Utility teapot with brown Rockingham glaze.

1962–63
Stoneware teapot with 'Arabesque' pattern by Gill Pemberton for Denby Pottery, England.

Burleigh Blue Calico earthenware teapot.

Queensbury Hunt for John Lewis
Cuisine teapot.

Teapot from Jansen + Co, a Dutch firm
based in Amsterdam and founded by
Anouk Jansen and Harm Magis.

Joules porcelain teapot.

Butterfly Bloom, a Wedgwood design
based on patterns from the company
archives, Stoke-on-Trent, Staffordshire.

Le Creuset Grand, enamelled cast-
iron design from the famous French
foundry at Fresnoy-le-Grand, Picardy.

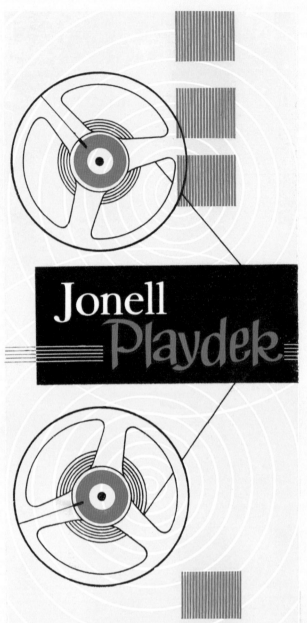

Vintage 1960s advertisements for John Lewis Jonell-brand audio equipment.

An excellent Value!

"*Jonell*" TABLE MODEL

★ High in Quality   ★ Low in Cost !

A five valve super-heterodyne circuit for A.C. Mains (200/250): Three Wavebands: Long, Medium & Short; Four point tone control; Illuminated dial with station names for easy tuning; Walnut finished Cabinet of good design 19" x 12" x 9."

Ask about our Maintenance Insurance Scheme, 12 months' free service and replacement of parts (including valves) from as little as 17/-

13 GNS or 28/- deposit and 24 Monthly Payments of 11/3

Also see the "JONELL" RADIO-GRAM at 39½ GNS.

Television
Demonstrations in the Department at Holme Moss transmissions—or in your own home if you prefer. Expert advice on the permanent installation of television.

Cole Brothers Ltd., Fargate and Church St., Sheffield, 1

COLES

The next revolution – one we are still undergoing – was in the widespread application of electronic, digital and communications technology in the home. The twenty-first century brought the flat-screen, high-definition plasma TV. The radio and television departments at John Lewis, as elsewhere, grew with the popularity and sheer physical scale of these new domestic 'gods'. Dwarfing even the old 1950s 'television sets', a TV screen today can cover an entire wall. In fact, the wall can *be* the screen, with programmes beamed on to it, giving everyone the chance to have a home cinema of their own.

What was amazing, however, was the growth of digital products, especially as prices fell at the lower end of the market. By 2010, many British homes boasted a flat-screen TV, while kitchens, living rooms and bedrooms filled with computers, music systems and mobile phones. This

The larger image below shows
an original 1964 GPO 712-model
Trimphone designed by Martyn
Rowlands. A copy of this and a
retro-style 1967 GPO 746 model
(shown at the top of the page)
are sold by John Lewis today.

in itself was a fascinating turn of design events. Where, for example, our affluent seventeenth-century forebears would display their wealth through magnificently wrought tapestries, today, expensive household appliances are sometimes employed to the same purpose. This partly demonstrates why design museums have become popular in affluent countries: they recognize that Philippe Starck lemon squeezers and James Dyson vacuum cleaners are works of art in their own right. Furthermore, when they see such objects on display in museums and galleries, consumers can feel they have invested intelligently in objects that are much more than mere appliances.

A glance today at any John Lewis lighting department sums up these extraordinary changes in the fortunes of household goods. For most of the late 1940s and the 1950s, there was little choice in this area. There were some

Secto Victo
Black ceiling light
by Seppo Koho.

BTC Titan
Ceiling light.

Flos Spun table lamp
by Sebastian Wrong.

Anglepoise 1227 lamp
by George Carwardine.

Harmony table lamp
for John Lewis.

nice lampshades and even anglepoise lamps for the daring (especially for the engineer or architect in the family, and still sold today). Most lighting, however, was from single tungsten bulbs hanging centrally from a ceiling and barely protected by small, dust-gathering shades.

Today, the choice is extensive. In the lighting department alone, customers can choose from hundreds of the finest examples from the past 50 years. Here are lamps by Achille Castiglioni, Jasper Morrison, Vico Magistretti and Philippe Starck – some of the most valued names in contemporary domestic design. And, if this is not enough, there are dozens of lampshades to choose from, many of them designed in-house by John Lewis itself. As for garden lighting, virtually any mood can be evoked through a galaxy of electric lights.

Catering to this ever-growing demand for well-designed goods and products, John Lewis has considerably expanded its own-brand ranges through collaborations with a number of renowned designers. The John Lewis Design Collective brings together some of the best designers to create a diverse but exciting range of homewares. You can now find John Lewis furniture designed by Nick Munro and Matthew Hilton, crockery by Queensberry Hunt, and carpets and textiles by Christopher Farr, to name but a few.

John Lewis is the perfect place to come for the recent revival of fabrics and wallpapers, and its selection is huge, whether the customer chooses from John Lewis fabrics or a whole host of designers. John Lewis's own-brand products have gone from strength to strength as British consumers

Artemide Tolomeo Mega Terra
Floor lamp by Michele de Lucchi
and Giancarlo Fassina.

Kartell Bourgie
Table lamp by
Ferruccio Laviani.

Joey
Touch table lamp by
John Lewis.

Flos K Tribe
Bronze table lamp by
Philippe Starck.

have developed a taste for 'designer' goods. Today, John Lewis's own brand offers more than 100,000 products. John Lewis believes – and the figures prove it – that own-brand products are a unique reason to shop at John Lewis. As Stuart Hampson, chairman of John Lewis, said at the time of the launch of the John Lewis brand, 'We want customers to have the same feelings about each John Lewis branded product as they have about coming into our shops. We must ensure that we demonstrate real pride in products which carry our name.' They nurture trust between retailer and customer, because John Lewis takes a long-term view of shopping, and the world. Customers thereby know that John Lewis will be here for generations to come, always taking an interest in the goods it has

provided for its customers – especially those sold under its own-brand banner.

Own-brand goods are sourced from responsible manufacturers and suppliers. Where possible, John Lewis supports British makers using 'proper' materials – for example, tweeds for men's jackets. John Lewis takes care of the production of goods – from spoons to suits – from the design stage through to their manufacture, transportation, distribution and sale.

John Lewis shops have, in fact, been stocking 'own-brand' goods for many decades in one form or another. And not just from Jonelle but also from unexpected sources, such as Odney Pottery.

There had also been beds and kitchen furniture at John Lewis from Taylor & Penton, a Partnership firm that had

BUTTON

John Lewis has long been known for its haberdashery department. Buttons shown here date from each of the sixteen decades of the store's existence.

UP

1860s

1860s

1860s

1870s

1870s

1870s

1870s

1880s

1880s

1880s

1880s

1880s

1880s

1880s

1880s

1880s

1890s

1890s

1890s

1890s

1890s

1890s

1890s

1890s

1900s

1900s

1900s

1900s

1900s

1910s

1910s

1910s

1910s

1920s

1920s

1920s

1930s

1930s

1930s

1930s

1940s

1940s

1940s

1940s

1950s

1950s

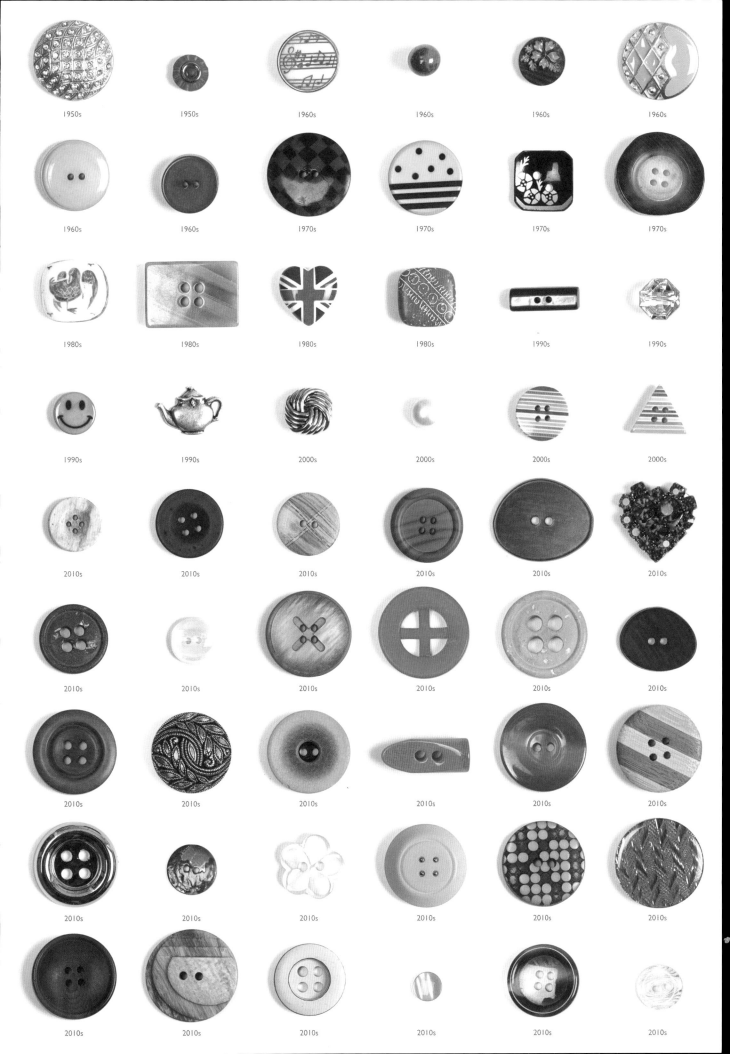

1950s   1950s   1960s   1960s   1960s   1960s

1960s   1960s   1970s   1970s   1970s   1970s

1980s   1980s   1980s   1980s   1990s   1990s

1990s   1990s   2000s   2000s   2000s   2000s

2010s   2010s   2010s   2010s   2010s   2010s

2010s   2010s   2010s   2010s   2010s   2010s

2010s   2010s   2010s   2010s   2010s   2010s

2010s   2010s   2010s   2010s   2010s   2010s

2010s   2010s   2010s   2010s   2010s   2010s

been started in Chelsea in 1935 before moving on first to Addlestone and then to Brooklands, Surrey. Although perfectly able to build Victorian-style beds, the factory was always up-to-the-minute, too. In the 1970s, it was busy making quilts. Brian Beamish, in charge of quilts at the time, remembers receiving an order for a 1.4 by 2 metre (4 foot 6 inch by 6 foot 6 inch) continental quilt along with one much smaller. When he queried the order, starting with the smaller quilt, the assistant who had taken the order replied, 'Oh, that is for Madam's poodle.'

There were fabrics from Birtwistle's of Lancashire, taken over by the Partnership in 1990, and lampshades from the Partnership's London factory, founded as Colello Ltd in Bond Street in 1925. Standards here were impeccably high. Ceri Guppy, a former manager with the business in its John Lewis days, recalled how work was so fine that stitches were invisible. 'Partners in the factory all had to be right-handed', she recalled in 2000, 'to ensure that they all pulled the silk the same way; and when I interviewed them I had to shake hands to see if they had sweaty palms, which would mark the material.'

WINGED FIGURE 1963
BY BARBARA HEPWORTH

6

AN
ENDURING
BRAND

2001–beyond

The twenty-first century began with the opening of the colossally expensive Millennium Experience at 'The Dome' in Greenwich. As memories of this Experience quickly faded, John Lewis successfully negotiated the new, intensely high-speed age of Internet shopping, 'brands', seven-day trading, roller-coaster economics, globalization, and a world of people seemingly glued to screens all day long – at home, at work and in public.

In 2000, Luke Mayhew, the newly appointed Director of Trading at John Lewis, asked an advertising agency – in focus-group mode – who John Lewis would be if it were a person. The reply was: a 50-year-old parish councillor with a moustache, dressed in blazer and grey flannels. While this was perhaps wide of the mark, nevertheless the company needed to push ahead with far-reaching and intelligent modernization to keep up with its business rivals. John Lewis was also compared at the time to other institutions perceived to be concerned with decency and fair play, like Radio 4 and the National Trust.

While there were things to change, people trusted the brand, and it was on this trust that John Lewis built. If it had been like most other companies – more driven by pure profit and a slave to the stock market – then it might well have refused to plough a massive £100 million into the refurbishment of the Peter Jones store on Sloane Square and to spend a further £65 million upgrading its Oxford Street flagship. But John Lewis had a soul – and a stern guardian angel in the guise of the abiding spirit of Spedan Lewis. It also had the vision, and importantly the money, to plan for the long term rather than for short-term gain. So, while moving into the twenty-first century, it refused to act ruthlessly, whether with its buildings, its heritage, the livelihood of its Partners or the loyalty of its customers.

John Lewis had launched its own website in 2000, selling a limited number of goods, but in February 2001 the company signalled an expansion of its presence on the Internet by purchasing the UK arm of an online company that specialized in electronic goods, office supplies and gifts. This enabled it to combine the well-loved John Lewis brand with the latest online know-how.

The Oxford Street store with Barbara Hepworth's *Winged Figure*.

From 2002 the family names of provincial department stores were replaced by 'John Lewis'. Only Peter Jones and Knight & Lee maintained their separate identities. This was part of a push to build the brand of John Lewis, coupled with investment in the development of its own-brand business, now with annual sales of over £1 billion. John Lewis own brand now stretches across all departments, including fashion, home and electricals. It was trust in the brand that made this possible. As managing director, Andy Street says:

> People trust John Lewis, for value, honesty, good service, and guarantees ... We found that 75 per cent of the population would trust John Lewis if it were a bank, which shows the confidence people have in us; obviously that's something we're very proud of but should never take for granted.

In order to support new ways of shopping a giant automated warehouse opened at Magna Park near Milton Keynes in 2009, with a second due for completion in 2015; together they will cover the area of 25 football pitches. Magna Park particularly was crucial in terms of the company being able to deliver on Internet shopping and to stay one step ahead of its rivals. John Lewis has continued to evolve the format of its stores, investing in three different types of shop: its existing department stores; the John Lewis at home stores, the first of which opened at Poole in 2009; and smaller department stores, such as those opened at Exeter in 2012 and at York in 2014. This flexibility of format allows John Lewis to sell in places that cannot support a larger store, while offering a larger product choice online. Customers' shopping habits are changing: they now shop in different ways, whether in store, online or both. Adapting to these new ways of shopping enabled John Lewis not just to weather the long recession that cast a grim shadow over the global economy from 2008, but also to thrive.

Below
The cover of the Partnership's *Gazette*, March 2013 celebrates the 17 per cent bonus.

Bottom
John Lewis at home, Poole.

Opposite
The alternative John Lewis way of doing business makes the headlines.

Despite the collapse of banks, rising unemployment, anti-capitalist protests and sudden dips in West End trading after such shocking events as the '7/7' London bomb attacks, in July 2005, John Lewis maintained standards set by Spedan Lewis in the late 1920s. Staff bonuses were still paid, as they continue to be. John Lewis was undeniably a commercial rock during years of rapid social and technological change, and economic turmoil. Other well-known high-street names vanished overnight. Senior John Lewis management in the twenty-first century sought to strike a balance between the co-operative virtues of the Partnership in a very different age, and a dynamic and profitable business.

When Andy Street took over as managing director of John Lewis in 2007, Britain and the global economy were on the brink of recession. And yet as Street – who has worked for John Lewis since leaving university in 1985 – says, 'we haven't just survived the recession: we've thrived'. How come? Street believes that in straitened economic times, people have looked anew at goods and shops that offer truly good value, and that shoppers, especially, are keen to know how the goods they buy are sourced.

Because of what had happened in the wider economy, John Lewis's attitudes to business and its Partners became a model for others. Increasingly the company was a source of fascination – and even inspiration – to politicians of all three major British national parties. Could the

£211M BONANZA FOR JOHN LEWIS

Workers get annual bonus worth 17% of salary

9-WEEK BONUS TO SHOP STAFF

John Lewis pays staff more than £200m in bonuses for first time

John Lewis's worker-shareholders praised by Nick Clegg

Clegg plans a 'John Lewis economy'

EMPLOYEE-OWNED COMPANIES THE WAY FORWARD, SAYS CLEGG

John Lewis defies Christmas gloom to post record sales

Sales at John Lewis bring some seasonal sparkle

'Bricks and clicks' fuel John Lewis surge

JOHN LEWIS PLOTS DECADE OF GROWTH

Is John Lewis the best company in Britain to work for?

Innocent and John Lewis break into poll of leading brands as ethics becomes good business

LONDON 2012

John Lewis was one of the official providers of the London 2012 Olympics. Not only were public and press areas at the Stratford Olympic Village kitted out with John Lewis furniture, carpets and fabrics, but also all full-size department stores had official London 2012 shops, starting with Oxford Street and then Stratford, with the remainder opening in April 2012. These sold official Olympics merchandise like mugs, sports equipment, clothes, homeware and even jewellery. While the Stratford store had amazing views of the Olympic Park, the facade of the Oxford Street store was draped for the occasion with an enormous and stylized version of the Union Jack with Olympics logo, as were Cardiff, Sheffield and Stratford City stores, joining in the national sense of pride in the Games. Partners volunteered to work for the Olympics organization in the lead-up to the Games to help ensure that they were a logistical as well as sporting success.

OXFORD ST.,
LONDON. W.1

Early 1920s
Handwritten script gave
customers a sense of
familiarity with the company.

JOHN LEWIS & Co.

Late 1920s
A new formality sets in.

John Lewis

1957
Painterly-style logo well
suited to stores specializing
in fabrics.

John Lewis

1960
Modernization in all things,
including the John Lewis logo.

150 years

1932
Flamboyance in an era of
economic depression.

1954
An American-influenced logo for
an era when US consumerism
was greatly admired.

1989
Classical with a Modern twist.

2001
Clipped Gill Sans for the
new millennium.

John Lewis branding (above) has changed with the times. This rich history has inspired some new products and the publicity for the John Lewis 150 Years Anniversary (opposite).

co-operative Partnership model offer an alternative to conventional private-sector companies and the delivery of public services? After all, John Lewis was not just popular, and trusted by customers and a wider public alike; it was also very successful. Nick Clegg, the deputy prime minister, went so far as to call for the creation of a 'John Lewis economy', in which employees are offered a greater stake in the companies they work for. The big question that arose both inside and outside the company, especially at the time of the 2010 general election, was why had so few companies followed the John Lewis model? The answers are many, but one of the key reasons is that most businesses and entrepreneurs, especially those who have built a company up from scratch, find the idea of giving up control – and the financial rewards that come with this – very difficult.

Significantly, the Partnership announced a revised constitution in 2009, a year after the world economy went into recession. Also at this time, the British public was becoming exasperated with what appeared to be the unstoppable rise of 'management' in Britain, and the ever-increasing salaries and bonuses that were often given even when companies were faring badly. The revised Partnership constitution underlined its fundamental purpose and duties. The new document declared that:

John Lewis

—

ADVERTISING

Given their later success, it is remarkable that the first John Lewis Christmas ad aired only in 2007, the elegant 'Shadows', where John Lewis products are assembled in a pile, their combined silhouette creating a snowy image of a woman and a dog. In the following year the ads began to feature their sequence of chart-busting soundtracks with a selection of products shown accompanied by a wistful version of the Beatles' 'From Me to You' and the tagline 'If you know the person, you'll find the present.' A 2010 ad for Never Knowingly Undersold (opposite below) showed the passage of a woman's life, backed by a cover of Billy Joel's 'She's Always a Woman'. In the 2011 Christmas ad 'The Long Wait' (opposite above), a young boy impatiently passes time before the big day, but all is not what it seems: in a neat twist of the traditional tale, the long wait of the title refers to the boy's impatience to give his parents their present rather than to receive his. The ad ended with the tagline 'For gifts you can't wait to give'.

Each year anticipation now builds to see what John Lewis will do next for its Christmas ad, it has almost become a Christmas tradition. As soon as the ad is released, it creates a storm across social media and much hype in the national press. In 2012 there were 3 million views of the Christmas ad on YouTube, with John Lewis trending worldwide on Twitter and overtaking Coca-Cola during the Christmas period as the most searched for brand name.

In 2013 'The Bear and the Hare' ad generated 170 pieces of media coverage in the first three days, and through the Christmas period there were 12 million views of the ad on YouTube, four times as many as the previous year. In addition, the soundtrack to the ad, Lily Allen's 'Somewhere Only We Know', spent three weeks at number one in the charts.

John Lewis has won many awards for its ads including the IPA Effectiveness Award, the Marketing Society's award for e-commerce and a Cannes Lion for Creative Effectiveness.

Opposite and above
From high street to high fashion: models show off the new John Lewis & Co. range in London 2013. The designers of the labels for the range searched the John Lewis archive, basing their designs on the company's original 1920s logo.

Below
John Lewis's Bringing Skills to Life scheme.

The Partnership aims to make sufficient profit from its trading operations to sustain its commercial vitality, to finance its continued development, to distribute a share of those profits each year to its members, and to enable it to undertake other activities consistent with its ultimate purpose. The Partnership aims to deal honestly with its customers and secure their loyalty and trust by providing outstanding choice, value and service.

John Lewis is strongly committed to supporting its broader community through a number of activities both at home and abroad. For example, its free primary-school education programme, Bringing Skills to Life, aims to inspire children and develop their imagination and practical skills for life. Further afield is the Cotton Connect programme which was set up by the John Lewis Foundation in 2011 as part of a wider scheme to help its suppliers. It has given over 1,000 farmers in India training in sustainable working practices.

Customers also know that at John Lewis everything on sale has been considered. As Andy Street says: 'We have never lowered standards to gain new business.' Furthermore, the distinctive commitment that it is Never Knowingly Undersold remains a unique proposition within the company today. Even in the age of Internet shopping, John Lewis will still match the prices of a high-street competitor, whether in store or online.

Added together, all these factors have meant that the business has grown rather than shrunk throughout the recession. By Christmas 2013, there were 30 John Lewis department stores, ten branches of John Lewis at home, and johnlewis.com. Online business has grown very rapidly indeed, accounting for a third of Christmas shopping in 2013.

While some businesses might feel that this boom in online sales should mean fewer shops, John Lewis plans to build more. Many people like to browse online for goods and advice, but customers still enjoy shopping as a sociable leisure activity and want to come into stores to get inspired, get advice from Partners and experience products. The strength of the brand has enabled John Lewis to become more than a department store: in 2006 the company went into insurance, and by 2017 it expects 10 per cent of its business to be in services beyond retailing.

For customers who come to browse and buy in the shops, this is welcome news, as it means that John Lewis will continue to stock an unusually wide variety of goods well into the future. We will still be able to walk into the busy Oxford Street store, where the business was founded 150 years ago, and buy a button for a jacket or shirt, a zip for a dress or trousers, or any of those small, everyday items that few other stores would dream of keeping in such variety. It is this full choice of goods, sold by well-informed Partners, that, aside from anything else, makes John Lewis special. It is a characteristic that takes today's stores back to the very start, when John Lewis himself offered a greater variety of goods than his rivals.

Today, the ranges in John Lewis are broader and more tempting than ever. The shops are lighter, brighter and more chic than before. And yet they are utterly distinctive. In the second decade of the twenty-first century, John Lewis remains a successful and much-loved business quite unlike any other. And it works. Echoing Spedan, perhaps we should compare the John Lewis Partnership to the bumble-bee, which, we have been told, according to the laws of physics, cannot possibly fly. But fly it does – and very well, too.

Signage for the Stratford John Lewis
is unwrapped against the backdrop
of the 2012 Olympic Stadium.

JOHN LEWIS SHOPS

A

Aberdeen – *opened 1989*

Ashford* – *opened 2013*

B

Bluewater – *opened 1999*

Brent Cross, London – *opened 1976*

Brixton, London – *Bon Marché, founded 1877, closed 1975*

Brixton, London – *Quin & Axtens, founded 1905, amalgamated with Bon Marché, Brixton 1922, sold 1949*

C

Cambridge – *formerly Robert Sayle, founded 1840, purchased 1940*

Cardiff – *opened 2009*

Cheadle – *opened 1995*

Chester* – *opened 2011*

Chichester* – *opened 2012*

Cribbs Causeway, Bristol – *formerly John Lewis Bristol, purchased 1981*

Croydon* – *opened 2010*

E

Edinburgh – *opened 1973*

Exeter – *opened 2012*

F

Finchley Road, London – *John Barnes, founded 1900, acquired 1940, closed 1981*

G

Glasgow – *opened 1999*

H

Heathrow – *opens 2014*

High Wycombe – *opened 1988*

Holloway Road, London – *Jones Brothers, founded 1867, closed 1990*

I

Ipswich* – *opened 2012*

K

Kingston – *opened 1990*

L

Leicester – *opened 2008*

Liverpool – *formerly G H Lee, founded 1853, acquired 1940*

Liverpool – *Bon Marché, founded 1878, merged with G H Lee, 1961*

M

Milton Keynes – *opened 1979*

N

Newbury* – *opened 2012*

Newcastle – *formerly Bainbridge, founded 1838, acquired 1953*

Norwich – formerly Bonds, founded 1879,
acquired 1982

Nottingham – formerly Jessops, founded 1804,
acquired 1933

O

Oxford Street, London – opened 1864

Oxford Street, London – T J Harries,
acquired 1928, closed 1960

P

Peckham, London – Holdrons, founded 1900,
acquired 1940, sold 1949

Peterborough – opened 1982

Peterborough – Thomsons, founded 1913,
sold 1956

Poole* – opened 2009

R

Reading – formerly Heelas, founded 1854,
acquired 1953

Reading – A H Bull, founded 1897, acquired
1940, closed 1953

S

Sheffield – formerly Cole Brothers, founded
1847, acquired 1940

Sloane Square, London, Peter Jones
– founded 1877, acquired 1905

Solihull – opened 2001

Southampton – formerly Tyrrell & Green,
founded 1897, acquired 1934

Southsea, Knight & Lee – founded 1887,
acquired 1934

Stratford City – opened 2011

Streatham, London – Pratt's, founded 1840,
closed 1990

Swindon* – opened 2010

Swindon Outlet – opened 2008

T

Tamworth* – opened 2011

Trafford – opened 2005

Tunbridge Wells* – opened 2010

W

Watford – formerly Trewin Brothers, founded
1880, acquired 1940

Welwyn – formerly Welwyn Stores, founded
1921, acquired 1983

Weston-super-Mare – Lance & Lance, founded
1907, acquired 1933, sold 1957

Windsor – formerly Caleys, founded 1824,
acquired 1940, closed 2006

Y

York - opened 2014

* = John Lewis at home store

INDEX

PICTURE CREDITS

Abbreviations:
b = bottom; c = centre; l = left; r = right; t = top

BAL = © Bridgeman Art Library
JL = John Lewis
JLP = John Lewis Partnership
LKP = © Laurence King Publishing
MEPL = © Mary Evans Picture Library
PC = Private Collection
SC = © Stapleton Collection
SSPL = © Science & Society Picture Library
SM = © Science Museum
V&A = © Victoria and Albert Museum,
    London/V&A Images

Front Cover: John French/V&A
Back Cover: JLP

Page 6 Bettmann/Corbis
7 & 8 JLP
9t Stourhead, Wiltshire/National Trust
    Photographic Library/John Hammond/BAL
9b Christie's Images/BAL
10 V&A
11 MEPL
12 Archives Charmet/BAL
13 SSPL/Getty Images
14 Michael Nicholson/Corbis
15 Hulton-Deutsch Collection/Corbis
16 Smithsonian Institution/Corbis
17l Illustrated London News/MEPL
17r Hulton Archive/Getty Images
18t The Francis Frith Collection/Corbis
18b & 19 JLP
20 PC/BAL
21 JLP
22 Bob Thomas/Popperfoto/Getty Images
23–25 JLP
26–27 Dover
28t Bruce Castle Museum/MEPL
28c MEPL/Alamy
29 Bibliothèque des Arts Décoratifs, Paris/Archives
    Charmet/BAL
30–31 PC/BAL
32 bilwissedition/akg-images
33t & b V&A/Alamy
34–35 V&A
36–37 Museum of London/BAL

38 JLP
40–41 Charles Phelps Cushing/Classic Stock/MEPL
42–43 PC/BAL
44–45 Museum of London/The Art Archive
46 PC/SC/BAL
47 JLP
48t PC/SC/BAL
48b Archie Miles/akg-images
51t JLP
51b Popperfoto/Getty Images
52–57 JLP
58 Ruth Hollick/Hulton Archive/Getty Images
59 Bettmann/Corbis
60–66 JLP
67tl PC/BAL
67tr © Estate of Andre Groult/Bibliothèque des
    Arts Décoratifs, Paris/Archives Charmet/BAL
68–69 Jewish Chronicle Archive/HIP/TopFoto
70–71 Hulton Archive/Getty Images
71 inset Popperfoto/Getty Images
72–73 Hulton Archive/Getty Images
74 Bettmann/Corbis
75 PA Photos/TopFoto
76–77 V&A
78–79 JLP
80–81 Brooke/Topical Press Agency/Getty Images
82–83 Hulton-Deutsch Collection/Corbis
84–85 Central Press/Getty Images
86 Time & Life Pictures/Getty Image
87 JLP
88tl F. Frith Collection/akg-images
88tr JLP
88cl Bedford Lemere & Co./Reproduced by
    permission of English Heritage/NMR
88b, 89 & 90t JLP
90b JLP
91 JLP
92l Lad Cuttings and Ephemera/London Borough
    of Lambeth
92r JLP
93t & b V&A
94t Ace Stock Ltd/Alamy
94cl, cr & b SSPL/Getty Images
96–97 JLP
98 Picture Post/Hulton Archive/Getty Images
99 Central Press/Topfoto
100–101 JLP
102 The National Archives/SSPL/Getty Images
103 Lebrecht Music and Arts Photo Library/Alamy

BIBLIOGRAPHY

Cox, Peter: *Spedan's Partnership, The Story of
    John Lewis and Waitrose*, Labatie, 2010

Kennedy, Carol: *The Merchant Princes;
    Family, Fortune and Philanthropy: Cadbury,
    Sainsbury and John Lewis*, Hutchison, 2000

Lewis, Peter: *John Lewis*, 2009
    [private family history]

Lewis, Peter: *Spedan Lewis*, 2013
    [private family history]

Lewis, John Spedan: *Partnership for All*,
    John Lewis Partnership, 1948

*John Spedan Lewis 1885–1963, Remembered by
    some of his contemporaries in the centenary
    of the year of his birth*, John Lewis
    Partnership, 1985

Collected volumes, *The Gazette*, 1918–2014

ACKNOWLEDGEMENTS

Picture researcher: Julia Ruxton
Designer: Alexandre Coco
Senior editor: Peter Jones

The author would like to thank:

Judy Faraday and Gavin Henderson at
the John Lewis Partnership Archive
Patrick Lewis
Peter Lewis
Sir Charlie Mayfield
Andrew Moys
Paul Porral
Andy Street
Louise Warren